# SPARK: IGNITE YOUR CONFIDENCE, POSITIVITY, AND MOTIVATION

## Unleashing Your Inner Light: A Comprehensive Guide to Confidence, Positivity, and Self-Motivation

### D.R. T. Stephens

**S.D.N Publishing**

# CONTENTS

Others

# GENERAL DISCLAIMER

This book is intended to provide informative and educational material on the subject matter covered. The author(s), publisher, and any affiliated parties make no representations or warranties with respect to the accuracy, applicability, completeness, or suitability of the contents herein and specifically disclaim any implied warranties of merchantability or fitness for a particular purpose.

The information contained in this book is for general information purposes only and is not intended to serve as legal, medical, financial, or any other form of professional advice. Readers should consult with appropriate professionals before making any decisions based on the information provided. Neither the author(s) nor the publisher shall be held responsible or liable for any loss, damage, injury, claim, or otherwise, whether direct or indirect, consequential, or incidental, that may occur as a result of applying or misinterpreting the information in this book.

This book may contain references to third-party websites, products, or services. Such references do not constitute an endorsement or recommendation, and the author(s) and publisher are not responsible for any outcomes related to these third-party references.

In no event shall the author(s), publisher, or any affiliated parties be liable for any direct, indirect, punitive, special, incidental, or other consequential damages arising directly or indirectly from any use of this material, which is provided "as is," and without warranties of any kind, express or implied.

By reading this book, you acknowledge and agree that you assume all risks and responsibilities concerning the applicability and consequences of the information provided. You also agree to indemnify, defend, and hold harmless the author(s), publisher, and any affiliated parties from any and all liabilities, claims, demands, actions, and causes of action whatsoever, whether or not foreseeable, that may arise from using or misusing the information contained in this book.

Although every effort has been made to ensure the accuracy of the information in this book as of the date of publication, the landscape of the subject matter covered is continuously evolving. Therefore, the author(s) and publisher expressly disclaim responsibility for any errors or omissions and reserve the right to update, alter, or revise the content without prior notice.

By continuing to read this book, you agree to be bound by the terms and conditions stated in this disclaimer. If you do not agree with these terms, it is your responsibility to discontinue use of this book immediately.

# INTRODUCTION: UNDERSTANDING CONFIDENCE, POSITIVITY, AND MOTIVATION

Welcome to Spark: Ignite Your Confidence, Positivity, and Motivation - a transformative journey into the realms of self-improvement, where we will unlock the secrets of these powerful forces that can change our lives.

We all seek to better ourselves in different ways, whether that be in our personal or professional lives, our relationships, or even in how we perceive ourselves. Despite our unique circumstances and goals, three core aspects significantly influence our journey of self-improvement: confidence, positivity, and motivation. They are the guiding lights that help us navigate the tumultuous seas of life, leading us toward our most authentic selves and fullest potential.

But what exactly are these three forces, and why are they so crucial?

**Confidence** is often defined as the belief in oneself and one's own abilities. It's the fuel that drives our actions, turning ideas into realities. A confident person not only believes they can succeed but also has the resilience to handle failure and learn from it.

**Positivity**, on the other hand, is the ability to maintain a positive outlook despite challenges. This isn't about ignoring reality or masking the pain with false happiness. Instead, it's about recognizing both the good and the bad, then choosing to focus on the good while learning from the bad. A positive mindset enables us to see opportunities where others see obstacles.

And then we have **Motivation**, the compelling force that pushes us to act. It's the drive that stirs within us when we set a new goal or dream a new dream. Motivation is the propeller that launches us into action and keeps us moving, even when the journey gets tough.

These forces, when nurtured, can usher us into a world of limitless possibilities. They make us resilient in the face of adversity, persistent when confronted with obstacles, and allow us to see opportunities even amidst difficulties. But, like any other aspect of life, these forces need to be understood, cultivated, and harnessed effectively.

In this book, we will embark on a 100-chapter journey to do just that. Through each chapter, we will delve deeper into various facets of confidence, positivity, and motivation. We will explore practical strategies, digest scientific theories, engage with compelling anecdotes, and participate in active learning through guided exercises and prompts.

From exploring the power of self-belief, embracing positivity, and cultivating a growth mindset, to mastering the art of self-motivation, each chapter serves as a mini-lesson intended to help you improve these aspects of your life. By the end of this journey, you'll have a comprehensive understanding of these three forces and a toolkit filled with effective strategies to keep your spark ignited, no matter what life throws your way.

Welcome aboard. Your journey to ignite your confidence,

positivity, and motivation begins now.

# CHAPTER 1: THE POWER OF SELF-BELIEF

The journey to igniting your confidence, positivity, and motivation begins within you - specifically, with your self-belief. Your faith in yourself and your abilities is the cornerstone upon which all else is built. It's the internal compass that guides you through the uncertainties of life and the fuel that powers your motivation to chase your dreams, face challenges, and, ultimately, transform your life.

The concept of self-belief extends beyond just having a positive outlook. It involves acknowledging your potential, understanding your capabilities, and recognizing that you possess the resilience and strength to overcome adversity.

In the realm of self-belief, you don't simply exist - you thrive, bloom, and reach for the stars. You become the master of your narrative, the hero of your life's story.

## Belief Dictates Action

Imagine standing at the periphery of a vast field, with your goal all the way on the other side. If you genuinely believe that you can reach the other side, you would likely take those first steps forward with resolve, tackling any obstacles that come your way. If, however, you harbor doubts about your ability to traverse the field, you might hesitate or even turn back.

This analogy exemplifies how our beliefs influence our actions.

When you believe in yourself, you're more likely to take risks, push your limits, and keep going even when the going gets tough.

## Self-Belief and Confidence: Two Sides of the Same Coin

Self-belief and confidence are intricately connected. While self-belief is trust in your capabilities, confidence is the manifestation of this trust. When you believe in your ability to achieve a task, your confidence shines through, making you more likely to succeed.

## Cultivating Self-Belief

So, how can one cultivate self-belief?

- Firstly, identify and celebrate your strengths. Recognize the unique skills, talents, and experiences that make you who you are. Nobody is you, and that in itself is a strength.
- Secondly, remember your successes. It's easy to forget about past victories, but they serve as proof of your abilities.
- Thirdly, surround yourself with positive influences. People who believe in you can bolster your own self-belief.
- Lastly, practice self-compassion. Understand that mistakes are part of growth, and forgive yourself when things don't go as planned.

Remember, self-belief is a journey, not a destination. It's a muscle you have to keep exercising. So, take that first step today and believe in your ability to ignite the spark within.

As we progress through the other chapters of this book, we'll explore more techniques, strategies, and insights that will help reinforce and expand your self-belief.

This chapter is just the beginning of your journey. As we progress, you'll learn to harness the power of positivity, motivate yourself to chase your dreams, and build a resilient, confident, and joy-filled life. In every chapter, remember that your belief in yourself sets the stage for your success. So, ignite your spark, and let's embark on this journey together.

# CHAPTER 2: VISUALIZATION: SEE IT TO BE IT

Visualization – it's a word we often hear, but what does it truly mean? More importantly, how can it impact your journey toward confidence, positivity, and motivation?

Simply put, visualization is the practice of creating vivid, positive mental images to reinforce your goals, hopes, and dreams. These pictures in your mind can act as a roadmap, guiding you toward the reality you desire.

This chapter will delve into the world of visualization, exploring its power, its science, and its practical applications in daily life. You will learn the specific ins and outs of this transformative practice and understand why countless successful individuals across a spectrum of fields – from athletes to entrepreneurs – swear by it.

## The Power of Visualization

Visualization is not wishful thinking or daydreaming. It is a purposeful, intentional activity with a direct impact on your brain. Research in neuroscience has shown that the brain cannot distinguish between real and imagined events. When you visualize, your brain fires the same neurons as it would if you were experiencing the event in reality. Over time, this "neuroplasticity" can physically change your brain, helping you develop new habits, attitudes, and responses.

## Practical Ways to Visualize

How can you apply visualization to foster confidence, positivity, and motivation in your life? The beauty of visualization lies in its simplicity and adaptability. Whether you're envisioning yourself acing a job interview or imagining the exhilaration of achieving a personal milestone, the process remains the same.

Here's a step-by-step guide:
**Define Your Goal**: Get clear on what you want to achieve. The more specific, the better.
**Relax Your Mind and Body:** Find a quiet, comfortable and peaceful space where you can focus without distractions.
**Close Your Eyes and Picture Your Goal**: Imagine the situation in as much detail as possible. Use all your senses. How does the scene look, sound, feel, and even smell?
**Feel the Emotion**: Engage with the emotions that achieving your goal would bring. Let yourself feel the excitement, joy, and satisfaction.
**Repeat Regularly**: Consistency is vital. Make visualization a part of your daily routine, like meditation or exercise.

## Visualizing Your Way to a More Confident, Positive, and Motivated You

Through regular visualization, you can mentally rehearse your path to success. With each mental repetition, your self-belief, positivity, and motivation can grow stronger. You'll begin to perceive obstacles as temporary hurdles rather than insurmountable barriers, your fears will give way to a sense of anticipation, and your doubts will be replaced by an unwavering belief in your capabilities.

Remember, when you "See It To Be It," you're doing more than just dreaming; you're laying down the cognitive groundwork that can bring your dream to life.

As we delve deeper into the later chapters, we will expand on this technique, tailoring it to specific goals and challenges. For now, let's bask in the immense potential that visualization offers and look forward to the journey ahead. Because as we will learn in our next chapter, embracing positivity is a powerful next step on this path toward igniting your personal spark.

# CHAPTER 3: EMBRACING POSITIVITY

In the pursuit of confidence, positivity, and motivation, embracing positivity is like the magical key that unlocks countless opportunities, not only in your perception of the world but also in your tangible experiences. Imagine positivity as the colors in a painting; without it, the world would be a grayscale. Positivity is the palette that adds vibrancy, depth, and intrigue to the canvas of life.

To some, positivity might seem like an elusive concept, intangible and vague. However, it's a state of mind, an outlook, a choice. Remember that positivity isn't about ignoring life's difficulties. It's about meeting them with an optimistic attitude, choosing to see opportunity instead of setback, growth instead of stagnation, hope instead of despair.

The first step towards embracing positivity is the understanding that our thoughts influence our realities. Just as a lens determines what a photographer captures, our thoughts shape our perception of the world. Negative thinking can obscure opportunities, discourage us from action, and distort reality. On the other hand, positive thinking encourages resilience, inspires action, and creates a supportive internal dialogue.

The challenge is to consistently choose positivity, especially during hardships. To do so, you need to practice, like a musician mastering an instrument. You must tune your mind, train it, and redirect it when it strays off course. It is not about ignoring the negativity in your life but reframing it in a way that focuses on potential growth and lessons to be learned.

For instance, when you encounter a difficult situation, instead of thinking, "I can't handle this," reframe it to, "This is challenging, but I can overcome it." This reframing allows you to shift from a victim mentality to a problem-solving mindset.

To help reinforce positivity, consider practicing gratitude daily. Recognize and appreciate the good things in your life, no matter how small or trivial they may seem. This act can train your mind to naturally gravitate towards positive thoughts, further promoting optimism and resilience.

Furthermore, surround yourself with positive influences. The company we keep can profoundly impact our mindset. Choose to spend time with those who uplift you, inspire you, and help you see the brighter side of life.

While embracing positivity may feel unnatural or forced at first, remember that it's a journey. Over time, it will become more intuitive as your mind acclimates to this healthier perspective.

### Exercise: Positive Perspective

*Now, as an exercise to encourage active learning, take a moment to think about a challenging event in your life. Write it down, and then try to reframe it from a positive perspective. What lessons did it teach you? How has it contributed to your growth?*

As we continue our journey through this book, remember that the ultimate goal is not to eliminate all negative thoughts. Instead, it's about fostering a mindset that allows you to acknowledge negativity without letting it dictate your life.

As we move forward, let positivity be your guiding light, illuminating your path toward a more confident, motivated, and fulfilled life. Embrace positivity, and you'll find yourself not only sparking your inner light but also radiating it, influencing the world around you positively.

# CHAPTER 4: THE GROWTH MINDSET

"The only thing that is constant is change." - Heraclitus.

In the world of self-improvement and personal development, the concept of a 'growth mindset' has been a revolutionary approach that reshaped our understanding of ability and intelligence. As we progress in our journey of igniting confidence, positivity, and motivation, it's essential to learn how to cultivate a growth mindset.

The term 'growth mindset' was first coined by psychologist Carol Dweck in her pioneering research exploring how our beliefs about intelligence can impact our success. In contrast to a 'fixed mindset' where individuals believe their intelligence, wisdom and talents are static, fixed traits, those with a 'growth mindset' perceive abilities as malleable. They understand that they can develop their intelligence, skills, and talents over time through effort, effective strategies, and guidance from others.

A growth mindset is the belief in your capacity to grow. It's about understanding that your brain is like a muscle—the more you use it, the stronger it gets. Embracing this perspective will empower you to step out of your comfort zone, take on new challenges, and turn failures into opportunities for learning and development.

Now that we've covered the basics, let's dive into three practical steps to foster a growth mindset:

**Embrace Challenges and Persevere, Regardless of Setbacks:** If you've ever given up on a task because it was too challenging or avoided one for fear of failure, you've experienced the limitations of a fixed mindset. With a growth mindset, however, you will come to see challenges not as insurmountable obstacles but as opportunities to improve and learn. When you encounter a setback, instead of admitting defeat, ask yourself: "What can I learn from this? How can I improve?"

**Cultivate a Passion for Learning**: Growth-minded individuals have an insatiable curiosity and love of learning. They are not merely interested in the end result; they relish the process of learning and improving. To cultivate this passion, seek out new experiences and opportunities to learn. This might mean taking up a new hobby, pursuing a challenging project at work, or learning a new language.

**Celebrate Effort and Progress, Not Just Results**: If we only applaud ourselves when we succeed, we risk fostering a fixed mindset. Instead, learn to value the effort, dedication, and progress that go into achieving a goal. Recognize that every step you take towards your goal, no matter how small, is a victory in itself. This shift in perspective will make the journey toward your goals more enjoyable and less stressful.

As we close this chapter, remember that cultivating a growth mindset is not a one-time event but a continuous process. It's about embracing change, seeking out new experiences, and seeing the potential for development in every challenge.

## Exercise: Growth Mindset

*To aid in this process, here's a thought exercise for you: Reflect on a time when you faced a significant challenge or setback. How did you respond? What could you have done differently if you had approached the situation with a growth mindset?*

By embracing a growth mindset, you're not only fostering an environment of lifelong learning but also stoking the fires of your confidence, positivity, and motivation. Remember, growth and comfort rarely coexist. So, step forward and out of your comfort zone, embrace the power of yet, and let your mindset be your springboard to success.

"The mind is just like a muscle – the more you exercise it, the stronger it gets and the more it can expand." - Idowu Koyenikan.

# CHAPTER 5: THE ART OF SELF-MOTIVATION

"Motivation will almost always beat mere talent." – Norman R. Augustine.

In this pursuit of confidence, positivity, and motivation, we now arrive at a critical crossroads. Until now, we have explored how belief in oneself, the power of visualization, the magic of positivity, and the essence of a growth mindset can give your life a new dimension. However, to carry these elements forth or give them continuity, we require something indispensable: self-motivation.

We all have days when we wake up with a spring in our step, ready to take on the world. And then, there are those when pulling ourselves out of bed, and performing even the simplest task, feels like a herculean task. What differentiates these days? You may guess it - motivation. More specifically, self-motivation is an internal drive that propels us forward even when external factors may not be favorable.

Let's understand self-motivation as the fuel for your journey toward a more confident, positive, and motivated version of yourself. In this chapter, we will break down the art of self-motivation, enabling you to carry this torch on your journey.

### Understanding Self-Motivation

Self-motivation is your personal drive to achieve, learn, and constantly improve. It's an internal force that keeps you on track, encourages you to persist despite hurdles, and drives you to reach beyond your comfort zone. More importantly, self-motivation keeps you going when external motivation runs dry.

Those with high self-motivation are typically more resilient in the face of adversity. They harness their passion, ambition, and initiative to keep their spark alive, regardless of external circumstances.

## The Building Blocks of Self-Motivation

Now that we understand the 'what' of self-motivation let's delve into the 'how.'

- **Set clear goals**: This step may seem simple, but is fundamental to self-motivation. Have clear, concise, and measurable goals, and understand why they matter to you. This clarity fuels motivation and propels you toward your targets.
- **Establish a positive mindset:** As we discovered in previous chapters, maintaining a positive attitude can significantly influence your motivation levels. Positivity allows you to see opportunities in obstacles and gives you the resilience to keep going.
- **Self-belief:** Self-motivation flourishes when you have faith in your capabilities. Cultivate self-belief, and you will notice a surge in your motivation.

## The Role of Intrinsic and Extrinsic Motivation

Motivation can be divided into two primary: intrinsic and extrinsic. Intrinsic motivation arises from within; it's driven by internal rewards like personal satisfaction, joy, or a sense of achievement. Extrinsic motivation, on the other hand, is fueled by external rewards like money, recognition, or fame.

While both have their places, intrinsic motivation tends to be more sustainable in the long run. It's the driving force that propels you forward, even when extrinsic rewards may be lacking. Find what intrinsically motivates you, and you'll find a more sustainable source of motivation.

## The Power of Visualizing Success

Remember the chapter on visualization? That technique can also help boost your self-motivation. Visualize the successful completion of your goals, immerse yourself in the feeling of accomplishment, and let this image motivate you to make it a reality.

## Exercise: Fuel Your Motivation Engine

*Take a moment to list down five things that truly motivate you, things that drive you to perform better, work harder, and aim higher. They could be anything from a personal passion to a broader cause you care about.*

Remember, self-motivation isn't a skill acquired overnight. It's a gradual

# CHAPTER 6:
# BREAKING DOWN
# BIG GOALS

"Great things are done by a series of small things brought together." - Vincent Van Gogh.

A big, ambitious goal often feels exciting yet intimidating. There's a thrill in setting our sights on something significant, but the enormity of the task can sometimes feel overwhelming. So how do we take those big, beautiful goals and make them manageable? Welcome to Chapter 6: Breaking Down Big Goals.

The answer to tackling big goals lies in the simple, yet powerful, process of breaking things down into smaller, actionable tasks.

Let's start with understanding what a big goal is. A big goal is a long-term objective that requires substantial time and effort. It's the kind of goal that cannot be achieved overnight or even in a week. It might be starting your own business, writing a book, running a marathon, or achieving financial independence. These are the goals that have the power to change your life.

When faced with such an ambitious goal, it's easy to feel daunted. You might think, "Where do I even begin?" The answer is: Start small.

### Creating a Goal Map

Every journey begins with a single step, and every large goal can be broken down into a series of smaller ones. Creating a goal map can be incredibly helpful. This is a visual representation of your main goal broken down into smaller, more manageable parts. Start with your end goal and work backward, identifying the steps necessary to get there.

### Set S.M.A.R.T. Goals

The S.M.A.R.T. acronym stands for Specific, Measurable, Achievable, Relevant, and Time-bound. By ensuring your smaller goals meet these criteria, you're more likely to stay motivated and succeed.

### Establishing a Routine

A crucial part of breaking down big goals is establishing a routine. Determine what small actions you can take daily or weekly to inch closer to your overall objective. Consistency is key.

### Celebrating Small Victories

Each small goal you achieve is a step towards your bigger goal. Remember to celebrate these small victories; they are signs of your progress and should be acknowledged and enjoyed.

Let's look at an example. If your goal is to write a book, it might seem overwhelming to think about the hundreds of pages you need to write. But let's break it down. Start with a simple outline of your chapters. Then, aim to write one paragraph a day, gradually building up to a page a day. Before you know it, you'll have a completed manuscript in your hands.

### Exercise: Goal Breakdown

*To make this journey more interactive, find a place in your journal or digital notepad for a goal breakdown exercise. Write your ultimate goal at the top, and then start to break it down into many smaller, manageable steps. Be as specific as you can. Each of these steps is a mini-goal that leads to your larger one.*

Breaking down your larger end goals into smaller tasks will not only make them seem more manageable, but it will also give you a clear path to follow. You will feel less overwhelmed and more empowered to tackle each task. Remember, it's not about getting everything done at once; it's about taking consistent, meaningful steps toward your goal.

So, as you move forward in your journey of self-growth, don't be intimidated by the size of your goals. Embrace them. Break them down. And celebrate your small victories along the way. Because every small step is progress, and every bit of progress takes you closer to your big, beautiful goal.

"Believe you can, and you're halfway there." - Theodore Roosevelt.

You've now learned the art of breaking down big goals. In the next chapter, we will explore how to overcome one of the most significant obstacles on the path to realizing our dreams - the fear of failure. We will provide strategies to shift your perspective and develop the understanding that failure is not the opposite of success, but a part of the journey toward it. Remember, every stumble is just another step forward. Keep your chin up and continue walking on the path of self-improvement. Let's march ahead, spark in heart, head held high!

# CHAPTER 7:
# OVERCOMING FEAR
# OF FAILURE

"Failure is not the opposite of success. It's part of success." - Arianna Huffington.

Have you ever felt so terrified of failing at something that you chose not to attempt it at all? It might even be that a fear of failure has meant that, subconsciously, you have undermined your own attempts to avoid the possibility of a more substantial failure? Fear of failure can be immobilizing, and if left unchecked, it can hinder you from achieving your goals. Welcome to Chapter 7: Overcoming Fear of Failure.

## Understanding Fear of Failure

Before we delve into strategies to overcome the fear of failure, it's essential to understand what it is. Fear of failure, also known as 'atychiphobia,' is when we allow that fear to prevent us from doing the things that can propel us forward to achieve our goals.

## Reframe Failure as a Learning Opportunity

The first step to overcoming the fear of failure is to change your attitude toward failure. View each failure not as a crushing defeat but as a chance to learn something and grow. Each failure is just a stepping stone on your path to success.

## Set Realistic Goals

One reason why people fear failure is because they set unattainable or unrealistic goals. Using the SMART goals strategy discussed in Chapter 6, set goals that are achievable and measurable. This can help reduce the pressure and the fear.

## Embrace the Unknown

Fear of failure often stems from fear of the unknown. Instead of fearing it, embrace the unknown. Accept that you cannot know the outcome of everything. The beauty of life lies in its unpredictability.

## Practice Self-Compassion

Being hard on yourself when you fail won't help you succeed. Instead, practice self-compassion. Remember that everyone fails—it's a normal part of life, and it doesn't define you as a person.

## Prepare for Different Outcomes

It's essential to understand that not everything will always go according to plan—and that's okay. Prepare yourself for different outcomes. That way, if you do fail, it won't be a devastating surprise, and you'll be equipped to handle it.

### Exercise: Reframing Failure

*Here's a little exercise for you. Reflect on a time when you experienced failure. How did you feel? What did you learn from the experience? How did it help you grow? Jot down your answers in your journal.*

Remember, as Michael Jordan once said, "I've failed over and over and over again in my life. And that is why I succeed." Every successful person has faced failure. But instead of letting it stop them, they've used it to spur them on to greater efforts.

So, don't let fear of failure stop you from pursuing your goals. Embrace failure as a natural part of the journey to success. After all, the only real failure is the failure to try.

In the next chapter, we'll explore the importance of authenticity and how living authentically can boost your confidence, positivity, and motivation. Always remember, the only person you should strive to be better than is the person you were yesterday. Let's keep igniting the spark within us and move forward on our path to personal growth!

# CHAPTER 8: LIVING AUTHENTICALLY

In the previous chapters, we've explored several building blocks of confidence, positivity, and motivation. One thing that underpins them all is authenticity. Living authentically means aligning your actions with your innermost values and convictions, no matter what others may think or say. It means being true to yourself, which can give rise to a more satisfying, fulfilling and joyful life. It also fuels our self-belief and motivation, as we're more likely to pursue our passions and aspirations when they come from a place of authenticity.

## The Importance of Authenticity

In an increasingly interconnected world, we are constantly bombarded with images and messages of how we should look, behave, or live. These external pressures can sometimes make us lose sight of who we truly are. However, living authentically isn't about fitting into a mold or living up to others' expectations. It's about being true to ourselves.

Authenticity has multiple benefits. It increases our self-esteem and self-confidence, as we're no longer trying to be someone we're not. It makes our relationships more genuine and rewarding because we're showing our true selves to others. And, importantly, it reduces the stress and anxiety that can come from constantly trying to meet external expectations.

## How to Live Authentically

The first step in living authentically is self-awareness. This means getting to know yourself deeply: your passions, beliefs, values, fears, strengths, and weaknesses. Reflect on your past experiences and what they've taught you about yourself. Practice mindfulness and take the time to listen to your inner voice.

Authentic living also requires courage. There may be times when your true self doesn't align with societal expectations or those around you. In such situations, it's important to stand up for who you are and what you believe in. Remember, it's your life, and you have the right to live it in a way that is true to you.

Additionally, being authentic means being honest and transparent, not just with others, but with yourself. This means acknowledging your mistakes and failures and using them as opportunities for growth and self-improvement.

### Exercise: Your Authentic Self

*To help you on your journey toward authentic living, take some time to complete the following exercise:*

*Define your values: What principles are most important to you? These could be things like honesty, integrity, kindness, or respect. Make a list of your top five values.*

*Align your life: How well do your daily actions align with these values? For each value, rate this alignment on a scale from 1 (not at all) to 10 (perfectly). If there's a value that isn't well represented in your life, brainstorm ways you could better incorporate it.*

*Reflect on your passions: What activities or ideas ignite a fire within you? These are the things you could talk about for hours that make you lose track of time or that you'd do even if you weren't getting paid.*

*Make a plan: How can you bring more of your passions into your daily life? Consider both small steps (like spending a few hours a week on a hobby you love) and bigger ones (like changing careers to align with your passion).*

Living authentically is not a destination but a continuous journey. It may not always be easy, but it is undoubtedly rewarding. It allows you to build a life that truly reflects who you are, bolstering your confidence, positivity, and motivation along the way. So, embrace your authentic self and let it shine brightly. After all, there's only one you in this world.

# CHAPTER 9: EMBRACING VULNERABILITY

"You are imperfect, you are wired for struggle, but you are worthy of love and belonging." These inspiring words by Brene Brown, a leading researcher on vulnerability, courage, and empathy, perfectly encapsulate what we will unravel in this chapter.

For many, the mere thought of revealing vulnerability provokes discomfort and fear. Society often frames vulnerability as a sign of weakness, promoting an invincible image of strength and self-sufficiency. However, in reality, vulnerability is a cornerstone of authentic existence. It's not about weakness or submission but about courage and transparency.
Let's take a closer look.

### The Misunderstood Strength of Vulnerability:

Vulnerability, contrary to popular belief, is not a sign of weakness. It is, in fact, a testament to courage. It requires bravery to expose our true selves, to risk judgment or rejection. It is in this space of vulnerability that we can truly connect with others. There is a profound strength in letting down our guards and stepping into the world with authenticity.

### The Power of Authentic Connections:

Authenticity breeds connection. By displaying our vulnerability, we open ourselves to truly connect with others on a human level. These connections are the bedrock of strong, meaningful relationships. It takes bravery to tear down walls, and yet, once those barriers are down, we have the capacity to form bonds stronger than ever before.

### Vulnerability and Self-Acceptance:

Embracing vulnerability involves recognizing and accepting our imperfections. It means acknowledging our fears, flaws, and insecurities. In doing so, we begin to develop self-compassion and, ultimately, self-acceptance. It's about being gentle with ourselves, accepting that we're not perfect, and understanding that it's okay to make mistakes.

### Vulnerability as a Pathway to Growth:

Vulnerability fosters growth. It's through vulnerability that we challenge ourselves, step out of our comfort zones, and truly grow. It opens doors to new experiences, new relationships, and novel perspectives that can transform our lives in remarkable ways.

### Practicing Vulnerability:

Practicing vulnerability involves being honest about your feelings and experiences. It's about being willing to share your true self with others, regardless of how they may react. It's about having the courage to express your needs, to ask for help, to say no when necessary, and to take risks even if they might lead to failure.

Now, it's time for self-reflection.

### Exercise: Expressing vulnerability

*Reflect on a time when you felt vulnerable. How did that experience make you feel? Can you identify any growth or positive outcome from that experience? Now, imagine how your life might change if you allowed yourself to be vulnerable more often.*

Remember, embracing vulnerability isn't about winning or losing; it's about having the courage to show up and be seen when we have no control over the outcome. It's about letting go of who you think you should be and embracing who you are. By embracing vulnerability, we ignite our authenticity, fostering deeper connections and empowering personal growth. Embrace your vulnerability. Ignite your Spark.

# CHAPTER 10:
# THE POWER OF
# AFFIRMATIONS

Affirmations, though simple in concept, hold a potent potential for change. These are positive statements that we consciously repeat to ourselves, helping to override negative thoughts or self-limiting beliefs. Used correctly, affirmations can become a compelling tool in your quest for confidence, positivity, and motivation.

### The Science Behind Affirmations

Before we delve into the "how," it's essential to understand the "why." Neuroscience has found that the human brain has a negativity bias. This means we are predisposed to notice and remember negative experiences over positive ones. Affirmations are one of the tools that can help shift this bias, focusing our minds on positive thoughts.

According to research, when we consistently affirm positive beliefs, our brains start to recognize these as our new reality. Over time, these thoughts can stimulate our neural pathways to create new, healthier patterns of thinking and behaving. That's why affirmations have been associated with lower stress levels, better academic performance, and even improved physical health.

### The Art of Crafting Affirmations

The secret to crafting an effective affirmation lies in its personal relevance and emotional resonance. Start by identifying an area in your life where you want to see change or growth. Perhaps it's your self-confidence, your ability to stay positive, or your motivation to pursue a specific goal. Your affirmation should be a clear, concise, and positive statement that encapsulates this desired change.

Remember, it should be in the present tense as if the change has already occurred. This helps your mind visualize and accept the desired outcome as your current reality. For example, instead of saying, "I will be confident," say, "I am confident."

### Practicing Affirmations

Repetition and belief are key when it comes to affirmations. Find a quiet moment in your day, perhaps during your morning routine or right before you sleep, and repeat your affirmation. Visualize the change, feel it, and, most importantly, believe in it. You can also write your affirmations on sticky notes and place them around your home or workspace where you can see them often. Another effective practice is to write in a journal, repeating your affirmation several times, as this can deepen its impact on your subconscious mind.

### Overcoming Challenges

You may find a voice of skepticism within you questioning the truth of your affirmations. This is normal, especially when you're working to override longstanding negative beliefs. When this happens, gently remind yourself that you are in the process of change. It might not reflect your reality yet, but it's a step toward the reality you are creating.

Affirmations are not magic spells that work overnight. They require patience, consistency, and belief. But with time, they can become a powerful ally, helping you reshape your self-beliefs and empowering you to spark your confidence, positivity, and motivation.

## The Power in Your Hands

By mastering affirmations, you are taking control of your internal narrative, and that is a significant step. It may feel uncomfortable at first, but remember that growth often happens outside our comfort zones. Your words have the power to shape your world. Use them wisely.

### Exercise: Mastering Affirmations

*Identify a self-limiting belief that you wish to overcome.*
*Write an affirmation that counters this belief in a positive, present-tense statement.*
*Practice this affirmation daily, following the steps outlined above.*
*Note any changes in your thoughts, feelings, or actions over time.*

Remember, the journey to a more confident, positive, and motivated you is a marathon, not a sprint. Take it one affirmation at a time.

# CHAPTER 11: THE BALANCE OF HUMILITY AND PRIDE

Life, in many ways, is a delicate balancing act. Often, we find ourselves at the precipice of two contrasting emotions, two seemingly opposing traits. The idea of balancing humility and pride is no exception to this rule. This chapter is a deep dive into this intriguing dance between humility and pride and how we can find the right equilibrium to fuel our confidence, positivity, and motivation.

Firstly, let's take a closer look at both terms. Pride, at its core, represents a deep satisfaction derived from one's own achievements, qualities, or possessions. It is a necessary component of self-esteem and a critical factor in maintaining motivation. On the other hand, humility is the ability to acknowledge that no matter our achievements or skills, we remain part of a vast, interconnected web of beings. It involves recognizing our limits and maintaining an open, teachable mind.

It may seem that these two are incompatible, but the truth is far from it. A healthy balance of pride and humility is the key to authentic confidence. This balance allows us to take satisfaction in our achievements without becoming arrogant, to recognize our worth without belittling others, and to maintain an openness to learning and growth without undermining our self-esteem.

Pride, in its healthiest form, can propel us forward. It's the pat on the back we give ourselves when we've accomplished a task, the silent acknowledgment of a job well done. It fuels our self-confidence and solidifies our self-esteem. But unchecked pride, on the other end of the spectrum, can turn into arrogance, which closes us off from growth and learning.

Humility, too, has its strengths and weaknesses. A humble person recognizes their own flaws and is always open to learning and improvement. They appreciate the input of others and see the value in diverse perspectives. But unchecked humility, on the flip side, can lead to a lack of self-worth or confidence, making it difficult to acknowledge and celebrate personal accomplishments.

So, how do we strike the right balance? It begins with self-awareness, the first step towards understanding your leanings towards pride or humility. Once we've identified these tendencies, we can consciously work towards finding equilibrium.

If you tend towards excessive pride, consider engaging in acts of service or learning about the accomplishments of others in your field. This can help you appreciate the broader landscape of your environment and encourage a more humble perspective. Practice gratitude for the opportunities and advantages that have helped you succeed, and remember to acknowledge the role of others in your achievements.

If you lean towards too much humility, to the point of downplaying your accomplishments, take some time each day to acknowledge your achievements. Keep a success journal, writing down all your daily victories, however small they might be. Practice affirmations that help to boost your self-esteem, and allow yourself to accept compliments graciously.

Lastly, remember that it's okay to oscillate between pride and humility. The balance may not always be perfect, and that's alright. The key is to be aware and make conscious choices that steer us towards a healthy midpoint, a place where we can be proud of our achievements and yet remain grounded and open to continual growth and learning.

As we continue our journey in igniting confidence, positivity, and motivation, maintaining the balance of humility and pride will serve as a steady compass, guiding us towards our true north of authentic, self-assured existence.

# CHAPTER 12: RISING ABOVE REJECTION

No journey to growth is complete without a few bumps in the road. In fact, some might argue that the bumps aren't merely an aspect of the journey but an integral part of the pathway itself. One of these challenging yet pivotal bumps is the experience of rejection. As we tread our path toward higher confidence, positivity, and motivation, we must acknowledge, understand, and rise above rejection.

Rejection is a universal experience; it's something we all go through at some point in our lives. It could be professional, in the form of a job we didn't get, personal, as in a relationship that didn't work out, or even societal, where we feel alienated or ostracized. And while it is a common experience, the feelings that accompany it are far from easy to bear. It's natural to feel hurt, disappointed, and even discouraged when we face rejection. But it's essential to remember that our ability to bounce back from these experiences will contribute significantly to our personal growth.

The first step in rising above rejection is understanding that rejection isn't always about you. It might seem personal, especially when it stings, but in many cases, it's not about your worth or value. Sometimes, it's about the other party's preferences, circumstances, or even their limitations. They might not be in a position to recognize or appreciate your worth, and while this can be tough to swallow, it's important to remember that it doesn't decrease your value.

It's also crucial to remember that every rejection is an

opportunity for redirection. Think of it as a signpost on your journey, nudging you in a different direction, possibly towards something better. Consider famous personalities who faced rejection before finding significant success: Walt Disney was fired from a newspaper for not being creative enough, J.K. Rowling's Harry Potter was rejected by twelve publishers, and Albert Einstein didn't speak until he was four, leading his teachers to think he wouldn't amount to much. In each case, rejection was simply a redirection to a path more in line with their true potential.

Another important aspect of dealing with rejection is not allowing it to define you. Rejection is an event or a series of events, not a testament to who you are as a person. You are not defined by the jobs you didn't get, the relationships that didn't work out, or the group of people who didn't accept you. You are defined by your resilience, your character, and your ability to rise above challenging circumstances.

Finally, it's critical to use rejection as a learning opportunity. This is where the power of a growth mindset, discussed in Chapter 4, comes into play. With every rejection, there's a chance to introspect, learn, and grow. What can you glean from the experience that can help you in the future? Is there a skill you need to work on, a red flag you ignored, or a pattern that keeps repeating? By analyzing and learning from your experiences, you turn rejection into a tool for personal growth.

### Exercise: Overcoming Rejection

*Let's end this chapter with a simple exercise. Think about a rejection you've faced in your life. Write down how it made you feel and the impact it had on you. Now, with the perspective gained from this chapter, write down how you can view it differently. What did you learn from it? What opportunities did it lead to or could lead to? How did it contribute to your growth?*

Rising above rejection isn't about denying its sting but about acknowledging the pain and then harnessing it to fuel your journey to personal growth. It's about transforming the negatives into positives and leveraging them to continue on your path to igniting your confidence, positivity, and motivation. After all, there is the old adaga that 'a smooth sea never made a skilled sailor', and in the rough waves of rejection lie the lessons that make us stronger, braver, and more resilient. In the following chapter, we'll explore the role of optimism in our journey of personal growth and how cultivating a positive outlook can help us bounce back from challenges, including rejection, and propel us toward our goals.

# CHAPTER 13: THE ROLE OF OPTIMISM

As we continue our journey of personal growth and igniting our confidence, positivity, and motivation, we arrive at the important aspect of optimism. The power of optimism, the conscious choice to see the world in a hopeful and positive light, can often be the unseen force that pushes us through obstacles, fuels our motivation, and aids us in achieving our goals.

Optimism is not about ignoring the realities of life or wearing rose-colored glasses. It is not the denial of challenges or hardships. Instead, it's the unwavering belief that despite adversity, positive outcomes are possible. It's the conviction that even in the face of setbacks and failures, there's always a way forward.

At the heart of optimism lies a key understanding: that setbacks and failures are temporary, external events, not permanent or internal conditions. This perspective is known as an "optimistic explanatory style," a term coined by psychologist Martin Seligman. Those with an optimistic explanatory style interpret negative events as temporary ("This will pass"), specific ("This is just one situation"), and external ("This occurred due to circumstances outside of my control").

Adopting an optimistic explanatory style can have far-reaching benefits for your mental and physical health. Research shows that optimists are more likely to maintain better physical health, have stronger immune systems, experience less stress, and live longer. Moreover, they are more resilient, recover from failures quicker, and are more likely to achieve their goals.

Optimism, however, is not innate – it's a skill that can be nurtured and cultivated. Here are a few strategies to foster optimism in your daily life:

- **Practice gratitude:** Gratitude can help you focus on the positive aspects of your life, fostering optimism. Start a gratitude journal, listing three things you're grateful for every day.

- **Use positive affirmations:** Affirmations are positive statements designed to assist you in challenging and overcoming negative thoughts. Craft your affirmations and repeat them daily.

- **Limit negative influences:** Be mindful of the negativity you may be consuming, whether it's from the news, social media, or pessimistic individuals.

- **Use optimistic language:** Try to incorporate positive language into your conversations and self-talk. Instead of saying, "I can't," say, "I'll find a way."

- **Visualize positive outcomes**: Visualization can be a powerful tool for cultivating optimism. Visualize yourself achieving your goals, overcoming obstacles, and thriving.

## Exercise: Optimistic Interpretation

*As a closing exercise, reflect on a recent setback or challenge you faced. Write down how you interpreted this event initially and how it made you feel. Now, try reinterpreting the event using an optimistic explanatory style. How does this change your perspective and feelings about the event?*

Optimism isn't about dismissing the realities of life or ignoring negative experiences. It's about choosing to believe that even in the darkest clouds, there is a silver lining. It's the lens that helps you see opportunities where others see obstacles and sparks hope where others feel despair. So, wear your optimism like a badge of honor, let it guide your way, and remember, the future is as bright as your faith allows it to be.

In the next chapter, we'll discuss the importance of building resilience and how it equips us to bounce back from adversities stronger and more determined.

# CHAPTER 14:
# BUILDING RESILIENCE

Congratulations, you have embarked on an amazing journey toward self-discovery, empowerment, and growth. Now that you have grasped the importance of optimism, it's time to introduce another crucial trait for our journey: resilience. Resilience is our ability to rebound from adversities and challenges. It's like an invisible shield that helps us stay strong, focused, and maintain our path despite the blows that life often delivers.

Resilience isn't about avoiding life's adversities; rather, it's about navigating through them. It's about harnessing the strength to accept these challenges, learning from them, and using that knowledge to grow. The truth is, life is not just about waiting for the storm to pass, effectively making you beholden to events, but about learning to dance in the rain. So how do we build resilience? Let's explore some strategies.

- **Embrace Change:** Change is an inevitable part of life. Instead of resisting it, embrace it. Remember, change doesn't always lead to negative outcomes. It often brings new opportunities and experiences that foster growth and development.
- **Acceptance**: Accepting the situation can help you focus on circumstances that you can change. Acceptance isn't about resignation or giving up but about understanding that some things are beyond our control, and it's okay.
- **Self-Compassion**: Be kind to yourself when things

go wrong. Self-criticism can be debilitating, while self-compassion encourages self-improvement from a place of love and patience.

- **Find Purpose: In times of adversity,** it's essential to hold on to a sense of purpose. It could be anything that brings meaning to your life and motivates you to keep moving forward.
- **Cultivate Optimism:** Maintain a hopeful outlook. Believe in your ability to cope effectively with hardships. Optimism is not about ignoring life's difficulties but having confidence in your ability to handle them.
- **Nurture Your Relationships:** Relationships can be a source of strength and support during challenging times. Reach out to your loved ones. Don't hesitate to ask for help when you need it.
- **Self-Care:** This cannot be overstated. Regular exercise, eating a balanced diet, and ensuring proper sleep not only improve your physical health but also strengthen your mental and emotional resilience.

## Exercise: Appreciating your resilience

*Now that you understand these strategies let's try a small exercise. Write down three challenging situations you've faced in the past. Beside each situation, note down what you learned from the experience, how you've grown from it, and how it has helped shape the person you are today. This simple exercise can open your eyes and understand your own resilience.*

Resilience, like a muscle, gets stronger with practice. It's not an inborn trait but a quality that we can develop. By understanding our capacity for resilience and cultivating it, we become better equipped to face life's adversities. Remember, it's not about how many times we fall but how many times we get back up and keep moving forward. Keep your spark alive and resilient because your journey is far from over.

As Nelson Mandela once said, "Do not judge me by my success; judge me by how many times I fell down and got back up again." Let your resilience be your judge and guide, always leading you toward growth and progress.

# CHAPTER 15: UNDERSTANDING EMOTIONAL INTELLIGENCE

The dawn of the 21st century introduced the world to a vital concept, one that has drastically influenced how we perceive success and personal growth. This concept is Emotional Intelligence (EI). In this chapter, we'll delve into the nuanced domain of EI, aiming to grasp its implications on our confidence, positivity, and motivation.

Emotional Intelligence is normally defined quite simply as the ability to understand, manage, and effectively express one's own feelings, alongside the capacity to engage and navigate successfully with those of others. It's a form of social intelligence that is based around the ability to monitor one's own and other's emotions, to distinguish between different emotions, and to use this information to guide one's thinking and behavior.

But why is Emotional Intelligence important? Shouldn't we be more concerned about our IQ levels and cognitive skills? The reality is that EI plays a substantial role in our lives. It impacts our relationships, decisions, and how we perceive and react to the world around us. It also holds an integral role in boosting our self-confidence, fostering positivity, and driving motivation.

Unlike IQ, which remains relatively stable throughout life,

emotional intelligence can be developed and honed over time. It's a dynamic entity that evolves and matures as we grow and learn. So, let's embark on this journey of nurturing our emotional intelligence, shall we?

Understanding your emotions and the emotions of others is the first stepping stone in this journey. Are you aware of what you're feeling at a given moment? Can you tell if a colleague is upset or if a friend is elated? This awareness helps us guide our actions, understand our triggers, and empathize with others, all critical aspects of personal and professional life.

Next, the ability to manage these emotions is crucial. It's not about suppressing what you feel but rather acknowledging these emotions, understanding their source, and directing them in a productive manner. This skill helps in maintaining a positive environment, even in times of stress and uncertainty.

Finally, utilizing emotional understanding to enhance our relationships is a vital part of emotional intelligence. We are social beings, and our success, both personal and professional, hinges on how well we interact with others. Being able to understand and respond to the emotions of others allows us to build stronger, more meaningful connections.

However, understanding emotional intelligence is just half the battle won. Let's try a simple exercise to gauge and improve our EI:

## Exercise: Self-awareness and Empathy

*Maintain an Emotion Diary: For one week, at the end of each day, write down the strongest emotion you experienced that day and what triggered it. Reflect on how you responded to that emotion and if there was a better way you could have handled it. This practice promotes self-awareness, a cornerstone of EI.*

*Practice Empathetic Listening: The next time you're in a conversation, try to focus entirely on understanding the other person's emotions and perspective rather than formulating your response. This active engagement helps you tune into others' emotions and fosters empathy.*

Emotional Intelligence is a continuous journey of learning and growing. As we ignite our Spark, let us strive to understand our emotions and the emotions of those around us, leading us to richer, more fulfilling lives. In the next chapter, we will delve into the transformative power of gratitude, a force that is closely tied to our emotional intelligence and can serve as a potent motivator in our lives.

# CHAPTER 16: GRATITUDE: A POWERFUL MOTIVATOR

Life presents us with an ever-changing kaleidoscope of experiences, emotions, and circumstances. Amid the hustle and bustle, we can lose sight of the good in our lives and allow negativity to seep in. In this chapter, we explore gratitude, a force often undervalued but incredibly potent that can act as a powerful motivator to drive you toward your goals.

Gratitude, at its core, is the act of identifying and appreciating the many positive aspects of your life. It is an acknowledgment of the blessings, large and small, that you receive each day. Yet, gratitude is not just about being thankful when things go right; it is also about finding things to be grateful for when faced with challenges.

We begin our journey towards embracing gratitude by understanding why it matters. Studies have consistently shown that practicing gratitude can significantly improve your psychological well-being, increase happiness, reduce depression, and enhance resilience. Not only that, but people who practice gratitude are also more likely to engage in physical activities, take care of their health, and have a generally optimistic view of their life.

Now, you may ask, "How does gratitude motivate?" The answer

lies in the way gratitude helps reframe your perspective. When you adopt a gratitude mindset, you begin to focus more on what's going right in your life rather than what's wrong. You start seeing challenges as opportunities and mistakes as learning experiences. This shift in mindset fills you with positivity, energy, and enthusiasm, all of which contribute to boosting your motivation.

So, how can you cultivate gratitude in your daily life?

- **Gratitude Journal:** Journaling is a proven way of fostering gratitude. Every night before you go to bed, write down three things you were grateful for that day. They could be as significant as achieving a milestone at work or as simple as a stranger's warm smile. Over time, this practice will train your brain to look for positive experiences throughout the day.
- **Gratitude Letters**: Writing a letter to someone who has positively impacted your life but hasn't been properly thanked can profoundly increase your sense of gratitude. You don't necessarily have to send the letter. The act of writing and expressing your appreciation is a therapeutic process in itself.
- **Mindful Meditation:** Practice mindfulness to stay present and appreciate the current moment. Too often, we are either ruminating over the past or anxious about the future. Mindfulness helps you to stay grounded and appreciate the 'now,' fostering a sense of gratitude.
- **Gratitude Reminders:** Setting daily reminders on your phone or sticking notes in visible areas around your house can prompt you to pause and think about something you're grateful for.

Remember, like any other practice, cultivating gratitude takes time and consistency. Start small and be patient with yourself. As you continue to practice, you'll find that gratitude becomes an integral part of your life, filling you with a renewed sense of enthusiasm, positivity, and motivation to pursue your goals. So, let's begin this journey of gratitude and unlock the enormous potential it holds to transform our lives.

# CHAPTER 17: THE STRENGTH IN ASKING FOR HELP

Many of us have grown up with the notion that we must be self-reliant to be strong. However, one of the most profound forms of strength is the ability to acknowledge when we need help and the courage to seek it. This chapter aims to emphasize the idea that asking for help is not a sign of weakness but rather a demonstration of strength and an essential component of personal growth.

There's a societal stigma surrounding the act of asking for help. Too often, we view it as a display of incompetence or a confession of defeat. However, recognizing our limitations and reaching out to others for guidance is a testament to our self-awareness and a crucial step toward overcoming obstacles.

Everyone, at some point in their life, needs help. That's an inherent part of being human. No matter how competent we are, there will always be challenges that we cannot face alone. By seeking help, we can tap into a wealth of knowledge and experience beyond our own. It allows us to learn, grow, and move forward more effectively.

The first step towards asking for help is acknowledging the need for it. It takes humility and honesty with oneself to admit when we are struggling, and it requires resilience to open ourselves up to potential vulnerability. You must remember that vulnerability is not synonymous with weakness. Instead, it reflects a depth of courage that empowers us to seek help when necessary.

Identifying who to ask for help is the next crucial step. It could be a mentor with a wealth of experience, a trusted friend or family member, or professionals who specialize in the area where we require assistance. Reaching out to the right person can provide you with invaluable insights and guidance.

When asking for help, communicate your needs clearly and honestly. Describe the problem you're facing, your efforts to resolve it, and why you think their particular expertise or perspective could be beneficial. This not only helps others understand your situation better but also shows respect for their time and knowledge.

In conclusion, asking for help is an act of strength and a sign of wisdom. It embodies the recognition that we don't have all the answers and opens the door to new learning opportunities and experiences. Asking for help isn't about being unable; it's about being smart enough to realize that we all need a helping hand sometimes. It's a key part of sparking your confidence, positivity, and motivation.

# CHAPTER 18: SELF-CARE: FUEL FOR YOUR JOURNEY

In today's high-paced world, it's easy to get caught up in the whirlwind of tasks and responsibilities and lose sight of our most crucial responsibility – taking care of ourselves. As this chapter explores, the concept of self-care is an integral part of maintaining and enhancing our confidence, positivity, and motivation.

Think of self-care as fuel for your journey. Just as a car cannot run without gasoline, we cannot function optimally without taking care of our physical, emotional, and mental well-being. It's not an indulgence but a necessity for maintaining balance and fostering resilience in the face of life's challenges.

Self-care is a broad term that includes and encompasses everything we do deliberately to take care of our mental, emotional, and physical health. It's about paying attention to your needs and taking the time to nourish all aspects of your well-being. This might involve physical activities, like exercise and proper nutrition, as well as mental and emotional practices, such as mindfulness and establishing boundaries.

A key aspect of self-care is recognizing that it's not selfish. Many of us are conditioned to prioritize the needs of others over our own, especially those of us in caregiving roles. However, taking care of ourselves is the foundation that allows us to take care of others effectively.

Common barriers to self-care include feeling guilty or a lack of time. However, a crucial point is that self-care should not be something we resort to only when we're already stressed, burnt out, or at our limit. Instead, it should be a proactive and preventative measure. By incorporating self-care habits into our daily routines, we can consistently replenish our energy and prevent burnout.

There are different dimensions of self-care, backed up by research, which suggest practical steps and strategies to take to create a personalized self-care routine and nurture your well-being, such as:

- Understanding the importance of quality sleep.
- A nutritious diet.
- Relaxation techniques.
- Hobbies.

It is also vital to set boundaries – a form of self-care that includes saying 'no' when needed and protecting your time and energy.

In conclusion, self-care is more than a buzzword or a luxury—it's a fundamental part of sparking and sustaining your confidence, positivity, and motivation. As you continue your journey, remember that caring for yourself is not just about surviving but thriving.

# CHAPTER 19: ACKNOWLEDGING YOUR SUCCESSES

One powerful source of motivation, positivity, and confidence is often overlooked - acknowledging your successes. This chapter focuses on the importance of recognizing your achievements, both big and small, and the transformative power this practice can have on your mindset.

Acknowledging your successes is about celebrating your progress and accomplishments. It's not about being boastful or developing an inflated sense of self. It's about recognizing that every step you take toward your goals, no matter how small, is a success in itself.

Why is this so important? Each success you acknowledge builds your confidence, fuels your motivation, and promotes a positive mindset. It's very easy to lose track of our progress when we're so focused on the end goal or what's coming next. However, by taking a moment to acknowledge what you've achieved, you can create a positive feedback loop that reinforces your belief in your capabilities.

Acknowledging your successes also allows you to reflect on what's working well and why. It provides valuable insights that you can apply to future challenges or goals. It also assists you in developing a growth mindset, focusing on progress and learning rather than perfection.

Yet, many of us find it challenging to acknowledge our successes.

We might downplay our achievements, attribute them to luck, or immediately move on to the next thing without pausing to reflect.

Ways to cultivate an awareness of your accomplishments might include keeping a success journal, where you regularly record your achievements or creating a 'done' list alongside your 'to-do' list to highlight your daily progress.

Celebrating your success can be done in numerous ways. Celebrations don't have to be grand gestures. They might be as simple as taking a moment to enjoy the satisfaction of a task well done, treating yourself to something special, or sharing your success with someone who supports and encourages you.

There are common obstacles to acknowledging success, such as the fear of appearing arrogant or the tendency to dismiss small wins. Through research-backed advice and real-world examples, later chapters will show you how you can learn to shift your mindset and start giving yourself the credit you deserve.

Remember, every step forward is an achievement. Every skill learned, every challenge overcome, every goal reached, no matter how small, is a success. By acknowledging and celebrating these moments, you can fuel your journey of confidence, positivity, and motivation. So, start acknowledging your successes today and let them be the spark that ignites your potential.

# CHAPTER 20: STEPPING OUT OF YOUR COMFORT ZONE

Growth lies at the edge of comfort, and no journey of self-improvement is complete without stepping beyond your comfort zone. This chapter emphasizes the importance of challenging yourself to take risks and explore the unfamiliar in order to spark your confidence, positivity, and motivation.

The comfort zone, that cozy place where routines reign and predictability comforts, may feel safe, but it can also be a prison of stagnation. Within its confines, growth opportunities are limited. When we step out, we open the door to new experiences, learnings, and self-discoveries. It's where the magic happens, where our confidence grows, our positivity expands, and our motivation soars.

Yet, the idea of stepping out of the comfort zone often triggers fear and resistance. It means facing the unknown and dealing with the possibility of failure. But these fears, while natural, should not be allowed to limit your potential. Embracing a little discomfort can lead to massive rewards.

First, it's important to identify your comfort zone. By understanding the boundaries of your comfort zone, you'll be better equipped to challenge them.

Once you understand your boundaries, you can gently look into ways to push these boundaries. This might involve:

- Setting challenges for yourself.
- Learning a new skill.
- Placing yourself in unfamiliar social situations.

The goal is not to leap unthinkingly into risky situations but to methodically stretch your limits in ways that contribute to your growth.

It is also important to learn the technique of being able to reframe your perspective, despite any discomfort and failure. Often, our fear of stepping out of our comfort zone is tied to a fear of failing. By learning to see discomfort as a sign of growth and failure as an opportunity for learning, you can reduce this fear and increase your willingness to take risks.

Inevitably there is fear and self-doubt that arises when stepping outside your comfort zone. Through evidence-backed techniques such as cognitive reframing and mindfulness exercises discussed in later chapters, you can learn how to manage these emotions effectively.

Stepping outside of your safe comfort zone might feel uncomfortable, but it's a necessary step toward growth, innovation, and self-improvement. By consistently challenging yourself in this way, you'll ignite your confidence, positivity, and motivation, pushing you further along your journey to your best self.

# CHAPTER 21:
# HARNESSING YOUR
# STRENGTHS

In the journey of igniting confidence, positivity, and motivation, understanding and leveraging your strengths is an invaluable asset. In this chapter, we focus on how to identify, harness, and nurture your unique strengths to empower your personal and professional life.

Your strengths are the tasks, skills, or abilities you excel in and enjoy doing. Harnessing them is not about ego or pride; rather, it is about acknowledging your natural talents and using them as tools to navigate the path to self-improvement. Each of us is a unique blend of skills, talents, and abilities. Recognizing and honing these strengths allows us to channel our energy more effectively, leading to increased satisfaction, confidence, and success.

However, identifying one's strengths can sometimes be a challenge. Society often compels us to fix our weaknesses while overlooking the power of playing to our strengths. To begin harnessing your strengths, you first need to identify them. Later chapters discuss how to use reflection, feedback, and formal assessments to discover your unique strengths.

After identifying your strengths, it's essential to understand how to apply them in different areas of your life, from work to personal relationships. You'll learn practical strategies to incorporate your strengths into your daily routines and long-term goals.

Yet, simply knowing and applying your strengths isn't enough. Like any skill or talent, strengths need to be nurtured and developed.

While strengths are a key aspect of personal development, relying too heavily on them can lead to complacency or a lack of growth in other areas. We'll discuss how to maintain a balance between leveraging your strengths and improving your weaknesses.

While it's important to leverage your strengths, it's also inevitable that you will sometimes need to perform tasks outside of your strength zone.

Harnessing your strengths is a powerful strategy for personal and professional development. By acknowledging and leveraging what you naturally do best, you can boost your confidence, increase your positivity, and foster your motivation, thus sparking a cycle of growth and success. Remember, strength lies in differences, not in similarities. Embrace your unique strengths and let them guide you on your journey of self-improvement.

# CHAPTER 22: UNDERSTANDING YOUR WEAKNESSES

Just as harnessing your strengths is integral to your journey of self-improvement, so too is understanding your weaknesses. A weakness is not a fundamental flaw but rather an area in which you might struggle or lack proficiency. Identifying and understanding your weaknesses is not about criticizing or diminishing your self-worth; rather, it is about self-awareness and growth.

Accepting that you have weaknesses, just like everyone else, can be a liberating experience. It can alleviate the stress and pressure of trying to be perfect and pave the way for personal growth. Once we identify our areas of weakness, we can begin to work on them, turning them into areas of potential strength.

You can identify your weaknesses through self-reflection, soliciting feedback from others, and self-assessment tools. By doing so, you create a roadmap for your personal and professional growth.

Handling your weaknesses doesn't necessarily mean turning every weakness into a strength; sometimes, it means learning how to manage your weaknesses effectively. This could involve seeking training or education, delegating tasks, or using strengths to compensate.

While it's essential to be aware of and understand your weaknesses, it's equally important not to dwell on them excessively. Overemphasizing weaknesses can lead to self-doubt and negative self-talk.

There is also a difference between real weaknesses and limiting beliefs, which are negative assumptions that hold us back from achieving our potential. It is important to learn, through reflection, how to differentiate between the two and how to overcome these limiting beliefs.

There are a number of benefits of embracing weaknesses, such as:

- Fostering empathy.
- Promoting learning.
- Encouraging personal growth.

Accepting your weaknesses can also increase your self-confidence as you realize that your value is not defined by perfection but by your holistic self, strengths, and weaknesses combined.

In understanding and accepting your weaknesses, you allow yourself the grace to be human, to make mistakes, and to learn from them. When seen from this perspective, weaknesses cease to be a source of shame and become stepping stones on your path to personal growth and success.

# CHAPTER 23:
# THE POWER OF
# PERSISTENCE

The road to confidence, positivity, and motivation is not always a smooth one. There are bumps, twists, turns, and sometimes, roadblocks. It's in these moments that the power of persistence becomes crucial. Persistence is the force that keeps us moving forward, despite challenges and setbacks.

This chapter will guide you on how to cultivate and harness the power of persistence to keep your journey of self-improvement alive, no matter what challenges you encounter.

We can begin by exploring the concept of persistence, its significance, and the role it plays in success. While talent and skill are important, research suggests that persistence—also known as grit—is often a more accurate predictor of success.

So, what kind of mindset is required for persistence? One that includes understanding that failure should be seen as not the opposite of success but a stepping stone toward it.

Persistence is an integral part of the concept of a "growth mindset," a belief that our abilities and intelligence can be improved, enhanced and developed with time, effort and perseverance.

Some practical strategies to develop persistence include:
- Setting clear goals,
- Developing a positive mindset,
- Building resilience

- Cultivating a support network.

In order to maintain persistence, we must also ensure we utilize self-care, as when we look after our physical, emotional, and mental health, we are better equipped to persevere in our efforts. Overcoming procrastination is another common obstacle to persistence. Some strategies to overcome procrastination include:

- Breaking tasks into smaller, manageable parts.
- Using time management techniques.
- Understanding and addressing the underlying fears or doubts that often fuel procrastination.

It is also important to celebrate small wins. Recognizing and appreciating progress, no matter how small, fuels motivation and reinforces persistence.

Lastly, let's address how to maintain persistence over the long run. It's normal for motivation to ebb and flow, but through specific techniques and strategies, you can continue to stay committed to your journey of personal growth. These could include mindfulness practices, maintaining an achievement journal, and regularly revisiting and revising your goals.

Persistence isn't about being stubborn or refusing to adapt to changes. It's about staying committed to your growth and improvement, adjusting your strategies when needed, and always moving forward, even if it's just one small step at a time.

# CHAPTER 24: BALANCING POSITIVITY AND REALISM

To truly ignite our confidence, positivity, and motivation, we must first understand that positivity and realism are not mutually exclusive. In fact, they are deeply interconnected. This chapter, "Balancing Positivity and Realism," is about finding harmony between these seemingly opposing forces to ensure our positivity is grounded, resilient, and productive.

Positivity is not about ignoring the negatives or glossing over problems with a veneer of false cheer. Instead, it is about focusing on the good, nurturing optimism, and cultivating a can-do attitude. Realism, on the other hand, involves recognizing and accepting the world as it truly is, complete with its ups and downs, possibilities, and constraints.

While positivity can uplift us and propel us forward, realism keeps us grounded. The balance between them prevents us from getting lost in over-optimism or pessimism. This balanced approach allows us to stay positive while facing the reality of challenges and setbacks, leading to better decision-making and more sustainable growth.

After establishing the importance of balance, we can explore practical strategies for maintaining it. This includes techniques such as:

- Practicing guarded optimism.
- Accepting and learning from negative experiences.
- Reframing our perspective.
- Using problem-solving strategies to deal with challenges realistically.

Realistic positivity can be used to effectively manage expectations, reduce the impact of setbacks, and make constructive decisions. Positive realism inspires perseverance and resilience, creating a strong foundation for confidence, positivity, and motivation.

Embracing reality does not dampen positivity; instead, it enriches it. When we couple a positive attitude with a realistic view of the world, we create a balanced mindset that is resilient, flexible, and deeply powerful.

# CHAPTER 25: FINDING INSPIRATION IN OTHERS

The journey towards igniting your inner spark of confidence, positivity, and motivation can often feel like a solitary one. However, it's important to remember that we are not islands. We live in a world rich with diverse experiences, triumphs, failures, joys, and sorrows. The stories of others can serve as a tremendous source of inspiration on our journey. This chapter invites you to embrace the power of connection and community and to find inspiration in others.

You've probably heard the saying, "You are the average of the five people you spend the most time with." While this might be an oversimplification, it underscores the important truth that the people we surround ourselves with can significantly impact our thoughts, behaviors, and attitudes. They can inspire us, challenge us, and drive us to strive for more.

There's a certain magic in finding inspiration in others. It comes from seeing someone else's struggles and successes, their grit and resilience, their pursuit of goals, and their journey of self-growth. This doesn't mean comparing yourself with others or trying to replicate their journey. Instead, it's about recognizing the human spirit in their stories and seeing what you can learn from them.

Remember, inspiration can come from the most unexpected places and people. It could be a close friend who always seems to handle setbacks with grace, a renowned figure in your field of interest who overcame significant adversity, or even a character from a book or movie who embodies qualities you admire.

To actively seek inspiration from others, consider the following:

- **Reflect on Your Role Models**: Think about the people who inspire you the most. What specific qualities or achievements do you admire in them? How can you incorporate these aspects into your own life?

- **Expand Your Circle:** Engage with a diverse range of individuals. Attend workshops, join clubs or communities, or volunteer. Different perspectives can broaden your horizons and spark inspiration.

- **Learn from Success Stories:** Read autobiographies, watch documentaries, and listen to podcasts featuring people who have overcome obstacles and achieved what you aspire to.

- **Stay Open and Curious:** The world is full of inspiring individuals. Maintain an open mind and a curious spirit. You never know who might inspire you next.

- **Share Inspiration:** Talk about the people who inspire you and why. By doing so, you not only reinforce your own inspiration but may also inspire others.

Keep in mind that finding inspiration in others isn't about idolizing them or putting them on a pedestal. It's about recognizing the qualities or actions that resonate with you and using that as fuel to propel you on your journey.

At the end of the day, your journey is uniquely yours. Others can inspire and influence you, but the actions you take, the challenges you overcome, and the growth you experience are entirely your own. So, as you draw inspiration from others, remember to honor your unique path and celebrate the incredible person that you are.

## Exercise: Inspirational Qualities

*Identify three people who inspire you and write down the qualities or achievements that you admire in them. How can you embody these qualities or work towards these achievements in your own life? Share your thoughts in a journal and refer back to them when you need a boost of inspiration.*

# CHAPTER 26:
# TURNING OBSTACLES
# INTO OPPORTUNITIES

As we flip to a new chapter of our journey, we take on a perspective shift of monumental importance. Every road to success is dotted with obstacles, but imagine if we could perceive these roadblocks not as barriers but as stepping stones to our goals. This chapter invites you to transform your mindset from seeing obstacles as impediments to recognizing them as opportunities for growth.

The first step in our transformation is understanding that obstacles are a part of life. Despite our best-laid plans, we are bound to encounter roadblocks that throw us off course. This is not a signal of our inadequacy or a reason to abandon our goals; instead, it is a part of the process of personal and professional growth. Our obstacles don't define us, but our reactions to them do.

Let's look at the story of Thomas Edison, the inventor of the electric light bulb. Edison faced thousands of failures before he made his groundbreaking invention. He didn't see these as failures but as steps on the path to success. Every unsuccessful attempt was an opportunity to learn and improve.

Next, let's learn to view our obstacles through the lens of opportunity. Think about a recent challenge that you faced. It may have felt overwhelming at the moment, but in retrospect, did it teach you something valuable? Perhaps it tested your resilience, taught you new skills, or helped you discover strengths you didn't know you had. If we train our minds to seek out these silver linings, we can transform obstacles into opportunities for learning and growth.

## Exercise: Identifying Opportunities

*Here's a practical exercise you can use the next time you face a challenge. Instead of asking, "Why is this happening to me?" ask, "What can I learn from this situation?" This simple shift in language can help reframe the situation from a negative to a positive.*

Moreover, sometimes obstacles can lead us to unexpected opportunities. When one door closes, often another one opens – sometimes, a better one that we may not have found if we had not been redirected. Obstacles can thus guide us to alternate routes that could bring us closer to our goals.

Lastly, obstacles offer an opportunity to practice resilience and problem-solving, key skills that are essential for personal growth and success. Every obstacle conquered increases our confidence in our abilities to navigate future challenges.

To summarize, obstacles are not here to hinder your path but to pave it. They shape you, strengthen you, and push you towards growth. By turning obstacles into opportunities, we can keep our journey towards success on track.

Remember, every stumbling block can become a stepping stone if you choose to step on it. Embrace your obstacles, learn from them, and turn them into your opportunities.

# CHAPTER 27:
# EMBRACING CHANGE
# AND UNCERTAINTY

In this new chapter of our journey, we confront two realities of life that are often feared and resisted: change and uncertainty. Although these can stir feelings of discomfort, they are intrinsic parts of life and growth. The key is not to avoid or resist them but to embrace and navigate them with grace and resilience.

Change is a universal truth. Life is dynamic, and everything from our surroundings to our thoughts and feelings is continuously evolving. Yet, we often resist change due to fear of the unknown and an inherent desire for stability and control. However, it's crucial to realize that without change, there would be no progress. Just as seasons change to give way to new life, personal changes often precede significant growth and transformation.

Start by acknowledging the inevitability of change and allow yourself to adapt and grow with it. A powerful way to do this is to reflect on past changes in your life. Think about how they shaped you and led to new opportunities. This retrospection can give you a more positive outlook toward future changes.

Uncertainty, on the other hand, refers to the unpredictable nature of life. While we can control our actions, we can't always control the outcomes. It's a common source of stress and anxiety, but when embraced, it can lead to increased resilience, adaptability, and personal growth.

One method to embrace uncertainty is to shift our focus from the unknown future to the known present. This practice is often referred to as mindfulness, which encourages us to stay present and engaged in the current moment rather than worrying about what lies ahead. It allows us to react to situations as they unfold, equipped with the skills and knowledge we have gathered till now.

In addition, it's helpful to cultivate an attitude of acceptance and flexibility. Acceptance doesn't mean passivity or giving up; instead, it's about acknowledging reality and adapting our actions accordingly. Flexibility, meanwhile, encourages us to remain open to various outcomes and routes to our goals. When we combine acceptance and flexibility, we can navigate uncertainty without being paralyzed by fear or apprehension.

## Exercise: Embracing change

*To help you embrace change and uncertainty, consider the following exercise. Reflect on a recent situation where you faced uncertainty or significant change. How did you respond? Now, imagine facing a similar situation in the future. How can you apply mindfulness, acceptance, and flexibility to navigate it better?*

Remember, it's not the most robust or most intelligent species that survive, but the ones most responsive to change, as Charles Darwin stated. Similarly, it's not the strongest or the most intelligent who will achieve their personal goals but those who can adapt and embrace change and uncertainty.

In summary, embracing change and uncertainty is not about eliminating fear or discomfort. Instead, it's about acknowledging these feelings and moving forward despite them. When we can do this, we become more resilient, adaptable, and prepared to take on whatever life throws at us.

# CHAPTER 28: NOURISHING YOUR MENTAL HEALTH

"Your mind is a garden. Your thoughts are the seeds. You can grow flowers, or you can grow weeds." – Unknown.

Welcome to Chapter 28, "Nourishing Your Mental Health." This chapter is a journey through the fertile landscape of your mind, a journey that is fundamental in sparking your confidence, positivity, and motivation.

Imagine your mind as a rich, thriving garden. The more you nourish it, the more it will bloom. However, ignoring your mental health, much like neglecting a garden, can lead to the growth of weeds - unwanted thoughts, anxieties, and doubts that hinder your progress.

## Understanding Mental Health

Mental health, in essence, is about your psychological and emotional well-being. It's about how you think, feel, and behave. However, mental health is not only about the absence of mental illnesses but also the presence of positive traits, such as self-acceptance, personal growth, and a sense of purpose.

## Nourishing Your Mind

To nourish your mind means to engage in activities that foster positive mental health. This could include physical exercise, adequate sleep, healthy diet, mindfulness, hobbies, and maintaining strong social connections. Consider these practices, such as watering, fertilizing, and weeding your mental garden.

### The Role of Self-Talk

The internal dialogue you have with yourself, known as self-talk, can either be a nurturing source of encouragement or a destructive force that plants seeds of self-doubt. It is crucial to monitor and adjust your self-talk, turning negative phrases into positive affirmations.

### The Power of Therapy

Sometimes, your mental garden may need professional care. Therapy can provide a safe trusted space to share your thoughts and feelings, gain insights into your behaviors, and develop coping strategies. Don't shy away from seeking help - a professional gardener always knows best.

### Setting Aside "Me Time"

Taking time to be alone with your thoughts and feelings is essential. This can involve reading, meditating, taking a walk, or even just sitting quietly. Remember, a well-nourished mind is more capable of fostering positivity, confidence, and motivation.

### Being Present

One of the most enriching fertilizers for your mental garden is the practice of mindfulness - being fully engaged in the present moment. It reduces stress, improves focus, and promotes a greater sense of peace and contentment.

### Exercise: Mindful Moments

*Take a few minutes each day this week to practice mindfulness. Choose an activity (e.g., drinking tea, walking, eating) and focus on being fully present during it. Notice the sights, sounds, smells, and how you feel.*

In conclusion, mental health is as important as physical health in your journey toward igniting your inner spark. Nourishing your mind is not a one-time task but a lifelong commitment that reaps a bountiful harvest of confidence, positivity, and motivation. Remember, every single thought you plant counts in the grand scheme of your mental landscape. Cultivate a beautiful garden that blooms with resilience, strength, and joy.

# CHAPTER 29: ASSERTIVENESS: SPEAK YOUR TRUTH

Welcome to Chapter 29, where we explore the power and importance of assertiveness. At times, the term 'assertiveness' may be misconstrued as being domineering or aggressive, but this could not be further from the truth. Assertiveness is about expressing yourself and your rights without violating others' rights. It's about standing up for your point of view while also respecting the rights and beliefs of others. Let's dive into it.

### The Balance of Assertiveness

Imagine assertiveness as the middle ground on a spectrum, where one end represents passiveness, and the other is aggressiveness. When you're passive, you remain silent, allowing others to violate your rights, perhaps for fear of conflict or a desire to avoid confrontation. On the other end, being aggressive means stepping on other people's rights as you strive to assert your own.

Assertiveness strikes the perfect balance, allowing you to uphold your rights while respecting those of others. It's not about 'winning' or 'losing' but about reaching a fair conclusion that acknowledges everyone's viewpoints.

### The Power of 'I' Statements

An effective tool in assertive communication is the use of

'I' statements. These statements allow you to express your thoughts or feelings without blaming or criticizing others. For instance, instead of saying, "You always interrupt me," you can say, "I feel disrespected when I'm interrupted during my speech." This not only fosters better understanding but also reduces the likelihood of defensive reactions, thereby facilitating healthier and more effective communication.

### The Role of Body Language

Assertiveness isn't just about the words you use. Your body language can often speak louder than words. An assertive stance means maintaining eye contact, using open body language, and speaking in a clear, calm voice. These signals show respect for yourself and the person you're communicating with.

### Assertiveness and Self-Esteem

Assertiveness and self-esteem go hand in hand. The ability to stand up for yourself and express your needs and wants is indicative of healthy self-esteem. Conversely, the practice of assertiveness can boost your self-esteem, as it reinforces the belief that your feelings, thoughts, and needs are valid and worth considering.

### Assertiveness as a Skill

Assertiveness is a skill, and, like any learnable skill, it can be honed with practice. It may feel uncomfortable initially, especially if you're used to being passive or aggressive. Like all skills though, if you take the time, are patient, and practice regularly, you can learn to express yourself assertively.

Start small, practice assertiveness in low-stakes situations, and gradually take on more significant challenges. Remember, it's okay to make mistakes. The important thing is to learn and grow from each experience.

### Exercise: Assertiveness Role-Play

*This chapter's exercise involves a role-play with a trusted friend or family member. First, think of a situation where you wish you had been more assertive. Share this with your practice partner. Now, reenact that scenario, but this time, respond assertively. Practice using 'I' statements and pay attention to your body language. Afterward, discuss how the interaction felt different and any insights you gained.*

*This exercise should provide a safe environment to practice your assertiveness skills and receive constructive feedback. It's a small step, but remember, each step takes you closer to becoming a more assertive and confident individual.*

In our journey towards cultivating confidence, positivity, and motivation, let's remember the importance of assertiveness. Assertiveness enables us to express our truth, fostering healthier and more fulfilling interpersonal relationships. As we wrap up this chapter, remember: assertiveness is not about dominating others; it's about honoring and communicating your own needs and rights while respecting those of others.

# CHAPTER 30: AVOIDING THE TRAP OF COMPARISON

We live in a world where the success, beauty, and accomplishments of others are just a click away. As such, it's easier than ever to fall into the trap of comparing ourselves to others. However, comparison is a dangerous game, one that often robs us of joy, confidence, and motivation. In this chapter, we will explore the pitfalls of comparison and learn strategies to avoid falling into this all-too-common trap.

## Understanding the Trap

Theodore Roosevelt famously said, "Comparison is the thief of joy." And he was right. Comparing yourself to others can often lead to feelings of inadequacy, envy, jealousy, and even depression. You might look at your neighbor's new car, your friend's promotion, or the seemingly perfect lives of celebrities on Instagram and feel that you don't measure up.

When you're playing the comparison game, you're often comparing your behind-the-scenes footage with everyone else's highlight reel. This skewed perception of reality can lead to a lack of confidence, positivity, and motivation.

## The Costs of Comparison

Comparison often comes with costs that we might not even realize we're paying. For one, it robs us of our ability to appreciate our own achievements. It can cause us to second-guess our worth and abilities. Additionally, comparison can foster a competitive mindset, where instead of lifting others up, we feel threatened by their success.

The other cost is the time and energy we waste obsessing over other people's lives. Every moment you spend comparing is a moment not spent pursuing your own goals or enjoying your own achievements.

## Strategies to Avoid Comparison

So how do we escape this damaging habit? Here are some practical strategies:

- **Practice gratitude:** Every day, write down three things you're grateful for. This simple practice can shift your focus from what you lack to what you already have.
- **Recognize your unique journey:** Remember that everyone is on a different path. Your journey, with all its ups and downs, is uniquely yours, and that's something to be celebrated.
- **Celebrate your accomplishments:** Instead of downplaying your successes, acknowledge and celebrate them. This can boost your confidence and reduce the need for external validation.
- **Limit your social media** use: Social media is a breeding ground for comparison. It is often worth considering setting limits on how much time you spend on these platforms.
- **Focus on self-improvement**: Instead of comparing yourself to others, compare yourself to who you were yesterday. This is the only comparison that truly matters.

## Embrace Imperfection

While we should strive to grow and improve, it's important to remember that we're all works in progress. You're not expected to be perfect. Embrace your imperfections and see them not as failures but as opportunities for growth.

In conclusion, avoiding the trap of comparison is not an easy task, especially in today's interconnected world. However, with a bit of practice and the right mindset, we can train ourselves to stop comparing and start appreciating our own journey.

Remember, your self-worth is not defined by how you stack up against others but by who you are, what you've overcome, and how you've grown as a person. That's what truly ignites your confidence, positivity, and motivation. And that's what will keep your spark burning brightly.

# CHAPTER 31: BUILDING A SUPPORTIVE NETWORK

A popular African proverb says, "If you want to go quickly, go alone. If you want to go far, go together." Our journey to ignite our confidence, positivity, and motivation is no different. In this chapter, we explore the essential task of building a supportive network around us.

No one succeeds alone. Even the most confident and self-motivated individuals need a network of supporters who can guide, inspire, challenge, and uplift them. These are the people who champion your cause, hold you accountable, and encourage you when times get tough.

### Recognize Your Current Network

Everyone already has a network, though we may not always see it. Think about the people in your life. Your family, friends, coworkers, and mentors all play a part in your journey. Recognize their roles and how they influence your confidence, positivity, and motivation. Are they building you up or bringing you down?

### Cultivating Your Network

Building a supportive network isn't about collecting people. It's about nurturing relationships with those who genuinely care about your well-being and success. It's also about diversity. A varied network can provide different perspectives, experiences, and skills to help you in your journey.

To cultivate your network, show genuine interest in others. Engage in meaningful conversations, listen intently, and offer help when you can. Networking is a two-way street where both parties have something to gain.

## Setting Boundaries

While building a supportive network, it's essential to set boundaries. Not everyone will support your journey, and that's okay. Recognize when a relationship is not contributing positively to your life, and don't be afraid to distance yourself from it.

## Leveraging Technology

In today's digital age, we're no longer restricted to our immediate geographic location when building our network. Leverage social media platforms, online communities, and networking apps to connect with like-minded individuals worldwide. Just remember that online interactions should be as genuine and respectful as offline ones.

## Network Is Net Worth

Remember, your network is not only about what you can gain from others. It's also about what you can contribute. Can you offer support, advice, or opportunities to others? Networks thrive on reciprocity.

### Exercise: Networking

*Audit Your Current Network: Write down the names of the people in your current network. Assess how each person impacts your life.*

*Set Networking Goals: Decide what type of people you want to connect with and how they can contribute to your journey. Be clear about what you can offer as well.*

**Reach Out**: *Start having more intentional conversations with people in your network. Show genuine interest, offer help, and foster deep relationships.*

Remember, a supportive network can be the wind beneath your wings, propelling you further than you ever thought possible. It's time to cultivate your network and allow your confidence, positivity, and motivation to flourish.

As we continue our journey in the next chapter, we'll explore setting personal boundaries—a crucial aspect of maintaining a healthy, productive network and an essential aspect of our personal growth.

# CHAPTER 32: SETTING PERSONAL BOUNDARIES

When we talk about confidence, positivity, and motivation, one often overlooked but crucial element is the establishment of personal boundaries. These invisible lines in the sand are what define your comfort zones in your interactions with others and the world around you. In this chapter, we'll delve into what personal boundaries are, why they are essential, and how you can go about setting them to bolster your journey towards self-improvement.

### Understanding Personal Boundaries

Personal boundaries can be defined as the mental, emotional, and physical limits we set for ourselves to protect our well-being and maintain our integrity. They're the ground rules for how we allow others to treat us and what behaviors we accept or reject. Think of personal boundaries as your property lines in your relationships and interactions.

### Why Boundaries Matter

Having clear boundaries is a critical aspect of self-care and self-respect. They are a sign of your self-worth, and they can help reduce stress, avoid conflict, manage your energy, and maintain healthy relationships. When your boundaries are respected, you command respect, and you demonstrate to others—and to yourself—that your needs, feelings, and desires are valid and important.

## Setting Your Boundaries

**Self-awareness:** Understand your comfort zones. Identify situations, behaviors, and interactions that drain you, make you uncomfortable, or challenge your self-esteem.

**Define your boundaries:** After you've identified what feels wrong, it's time to establish what feels right. Define what behaviors you will accept, how you expect to be treated, and what you are not willing to tolerate. These boundaries can span physical, emotional, mental, spiritual, and even digital spaces.

**Communicate clearly:** Once you've defined your boundaries, it's vital to communicate them clearly and assertively to others. Remember, people are not mind readers; they won't know your boundaries unless you make them clear.

**Be consistent:** Consistency is key in boundary setting. Regularly reinforcing your boundaries helps others understand what you expect from them and encourages respect for your space and autonomy.

## Overcoming Boundary Challenges

Setting boundaries isn't always a smooth process. You might face resistance from people who were accustomed to your past boundary-less state. Remember that it's not your responsibility to manage others' reactions to your boundaries. Stay firm, respectful, and empathetic, but always prioritize your well-being.

In conclusion, setting personal boundaries is a dynamic, ongoing process of self-exploration and communication. It's a brave step towards prioritizing your mental, emotional, and physical health—integral parts of a confident, positive, and motivated life.

## Exercise: Healthy boundaries

*As a practical exercise, take some time after reading this chapter to identify your current boundaries, evaluate areas where they might be too loose or too rigid, and develop a plan for enforcing healthier boundaries in the future.*

# CHAPTER 33: CELEBRATING PROGRESS, NOT PERFECTION

The quest for perfection is a siren's call, luring us into an endless cycle of striving, chasing, and, ultimately, feeling inadequate. Here in Chapter 33, we are going to shift that perspective and celebrate progress instead of perfection.

### The Illusion of Perfection

Perfection is an illusion, an unattainable ideal. When we become so entangled in chasing perfection, we often forget the beauty of progress. Each step you take toward your goal, each tiny improvement, and every small victory are the things that truly matter. They are signs of growth, markers on your journey toward becoming a better, more confident, positive, and motivated individual.

### Embrace Imperfection

In Japanese culture, there is a concept called "Wabi-sabi," which finds beauty in imperfection and transience. By embracing the imperfections in ourselves and our journey, we open up the possibility of authentic growth and true contentment. Embracing your imperfections does not mean you stop trying to improve, but it means accepting who you are at this moment and acknowledging your unique journey.

## Celebrate Every Step

Every step you take towards your goal, no matter how small, is progress. Celebrate it. Did you make a tough call you've been avoiding? Celebrate it. Did you start a new course to learn a skill? Celebrate it. Did you fail but managed to get back up again? Celebrate it. Every bit of progress deserves recognition.

## Changing Our Measure of Success

One way to foster this mindset is to change how we measure success. Instead of defining success as reaching a perfect end, let's define it as making steady progress. Recognize that every step you take towards your goal is a success, every lesson learned is a success, and every small improvement is a success.

## The Power of Yet

Stanford University psychologist Carol Dweck introduced a simple but transformative concept—the Power of Yet. It's about understanding that you may not have achieved your goal "yet," but you're on your way. You may not be perfect, yet you're making progress.

## Reflection and Recognition

Journaling is a powerful tool for acknowledging your progress. At the end of each day, write down what you did that moved you toward your goals. Write down what you learned, any improvements, and any steps forward, no matter how small they may seem. Reflection enables us to recognize and appreciate our progress.

## A Note on Setbacks

Setbacks are inevitable. There will be days when you'll feel like you're taking two steps back for every step forward. Remember that setbacks are not failures but opportunities for growth.

What's important is that you keep moving forward.

## An Invitation

This chapter is an invitation to let go of the pursuit of an unattainable perfect and instead embrace, celebrate, and be motivated by the progress you make each day.

### Exercise: Celebrate Achievement

*Write down a recent achievement or progress you have made, no matter how small, and celebrate it.*

*Start a journal to track your daily progress and the lessons you've learned along the way.*

*Reflect on a recent setback. What did it teach you? How did it contribute to your growth?*

*Celebrate your progress, not perfection. Remember, it is the journey of continuous self-improvement that fuels your spark of confidence, positivity, and motivation.*

# CHAPTER 34: ADOPTING A HEALTHY LIFESTYLE

The light of the day's first dawn was gently caressing the horizon when a prominent Greek physician, Hippocrates, claimed, "Let food be thy medicine and let medicine be thy food." While it's not necessary to dissect the molecular components of your lunch or dinner, there is an inherent truth in these words. Your lifestyle, especially your diet and physical activity, significantly impact your confidence, positivity, and motivation.

In this chapter, we explore how adopting a healthy lifestyle can transform not only your physical well-being but also your mental resilience, ultimately helping you ignite your inner spark.

## Nutritional Fuel

Often overlooked in the pursuit of confidence and motivation, nutrition plays an essential role in your mental and emotional health. What you eat, how much, and when significantly impacts your mood, energy levels, and mental clarity.

## The Mind-Gut Connection

The gut is often referred to as the 'second brain' for good reason. It's home to an intricate network of neurons and a complex microbiome, which influences our emotional states and thought processes. You can nourish your gut by eating foods rich in probiotics like yogurt, sauerkraut, and kimchi, which, in turn, fosters mental well-being.

## Nutrients for Mental Health

Nutrients like Omega-3 fatty acids, found in foods like fatty fish, flaxseed, and walnuts, support brain health. Magnesium, found in green leafy vegetables and whole grains, is known for its stress-reducing effects. Additionally, maintaining a balanced intake of proteins, complex carbohydrates, and healthy fats can regulate your energy levels throughout the day.

## Movement as Meditation

Physical activity is a powerful catalyst for confidence and positivity. Exercise triggers the release of endorphins, often known as the 'feel-good hormones,' which improve mood and energy levels.

### Regular Exercise: A Natural Mood Booster

Whether it's a 30-minute brisk walk, a yoga session, or a high-intensity interval training (HIIT) workout, physical activity reduces anxiety, improves sleep, and boosts self-esteem. Aim to incorporate a routine that suits your schedule, fitness levels, and preferences.

## The Power of Yoga and Mindful Movement

Yoga and other mindful movements like Tai Chi or Qigong foster a deeper connection between mind and body, enhancing your self-awareness and mindfulness. The blend of physical postures, controlled breathing, and meditation can significantly reduce stress and improve mental clarity.

As we explore a healthier lifestyle, remember that change is gradual. It's not about adopting restrictive diets or grueling exercise routines. It's about making small, consistent changes to your nutrition and physical activity that support your mental and emotional health. Whether it's swapping your midafternoon candy bar for a piece of fruit or incorporating a 10-minute stretch into your morning routine, every step towards a healthier lifestyle is a leap towards boosting your confidence, positivity, and motivation.

Remember the words of Lao Tzu, "A journey of a thousand miles begins with a single step." Start your journey today and spark a transformation that encompasses both body and mind, the physical and the metaphysical. Your journey towards a healthier lifestyle is not just about a number on the scale; it's a crucial part of igniting your confidence, positivity, and motivation. Start your journey today - your future self will thank you.

## Exercise: Lifestyle changes

*Make a list of three small changes you can implement in your lifestyle this week. This could be anything from drinking more water to adding a 15-minute walk to your daily routine or including more vegetables in your diet. Remember, no change is too small!*

# CHAPTER 35: DISCOVERING YOUR CORE VALUES

Living with confidence, positivity, and motivation isn't just about taking action and moving forward. It's also about knowing where you're going and why. This requires an understanding of your core values, the deeply held beliefs that guide your decisions, shape your behavior, and give your life purpose and meaning.

## Why Core Values Matter

You can think of core values as your personal compass, guiding you in the right direction when the path gets rocky or unclear. When you're in tune with your core values, your actions and decisions feel satisfying and authentic, propelling you towards a life that feels fulfilling and true to who you are.

Contrarily, when you're unaware of your core values or make decisions that clash with them, you might feel restless, unhappy, or unfulfilled, even if you're achieving success by societal standards.

## Identifying Your Core Values

The first step towards discovering your core values is to reflect. Consider the times in your life when you felt the happiest, proudest, or most fulfilled. What were you doing, and who were you with? What values were you honoring during those times?

Consider, too, the times you felt frustrated, angry, or regretful. What values were being suppressed or violated? Sometimes, we learn as much from discomfort as we do from joy.

Next, consider a broad list of core values. Here are a few examples: authenticity, balance, creativity, determination, empathy, freedom, gratitude, health, integrity, joy, kindness, love, mindfulness, novelty, openness, peace, quality, respect, sustainability, trust, unity, vitality, wisdom, excellence, youthfulness, zest.

From this list or from your own mind, choose ten values that resonate most with you. Write them down. Reflect on each and try to narrow down your list to five key core values.

### Living Your Core Values

Once you've identified your core values, the next step is to incorporate them into your daily life consciously. Reflect on your current lifestyle, relationships, and career. Are they in alignment with your values? If not, where can you make changes?

Setting your goals to align with your core values is an effective way to ensure that you're living according to what matters most to you. If health is a core value, for instance, you might set a goal to exercise regularly or to improve your diet.

Finally, be adaptable. Your core values might shift as you grow and experience new things. Regularly revisiting and reassessing your core values ensures they continue to serve as an accurate compass in your life.

### Conclusion

Identifying and living according to your core values is a powerful way to lead a life that's authentic and fulfilling. When your decisions and actions align with your core values, you're more likely to feel satisfied, content, and full of purpose, helping you to spark your confidence, positivity, and motivation. So, dedicate time to this process. After all, knowing and honoring yourself is one of the most important journeys you can undertake.

### Exercise: Your Core Values

*Reflect on a time when you felt truly happy, fulfilled, or proud. What value were you honoring during this time?*

*Now, reflect on a time when you felt upset, frustrated, or regretful. What value was being suppressed or violated?*

*Based on these reflections and the list provided, identify your top five core values.*

*Finally, think about one small action you can take each day over the next week to live according to each core value. Record these actions and commit to following through.*

Remember, discovering your core values isn't about choosing the "right" values but about finding the ones that are true to you. It's about understanding the essence of who you are.

# CHAPTER 36: CULTIVATING SELF-COMPASSION

Life's path is riddled with stumbling blocks, and we often end up being our worst critics when we fall. But what if we could switch that harsh inner critic with a compassionate friend? Welcome to Chapter 36, where we will learn to cultivate self-compassion, a fundamental aspect of building confidence, positivity, and motivation.

### The Foundation of Self-Compassion

Self-compassion, in essence, is treating ourselves with the same kindness and understanding we would offer a dear friend. It involves recognizing that failure, imperfection, and suffering are parts of the human experience that we all share. By embracing these, we provide ourselves with the warmth, comfort, and reassurance necessary to navigate through our toughest times.

### Understanding the Three Elements of Self-Compassion

Psychologist and self-compassion pioneer Dr. Kristin Neff identifies three elements that build self-compassion: self-kindness, common humanity, and mindfulness.
Self-kindness means being gentle and understanding with ourselves rather than harshly critical or judgmental. It involves responding to our struggles, mistakes, and failures with

kindness and forgiveness rather than self-criticism.

Common humanity involves recognizing and appreciating that suffering, unhappiness and personal inadequacy are shared human experiences – something that we all go through rather than something that happens to "me" alone.

Mindfulness is the clear seeing and non-judgmental acceptance of what's happening in the present moment. It allows us to observe our negative emotions and painful experiences without suppressing them or exaggerating them.

## The Benefits of Self-Compassion

Research shows that self-compassion is linked to numerous psychological benefits, including higher levels of happiness, optimism, and motivation and lower levels of anxiety, depression, and stress. Moreover, self-compassion promotes resilience, allowing us to bounce back from failures or challenging circumstances more effectively.

## Practical Ways to Cultivate Self-Compassion

To cultivate self-compassion, we must start by noticing how we talk to ourselves. The next time you stumble, pay attention to your internal dialogue. Is it harsh and critical, or gentle and understanding?

Here are some ways to foster a kinder relationship with yourself:

- **Practice mindfulness:** Mindfulness meditation or any activity that encourages a non-judgmental awareness of the present moment can foster self-compassion. By becoming more aware of our emotions without trying to suppress or ignore them, we can navigate life with greater ease and self-understanding.
- **Reframe your inner dialogue**: The next time you notice a self-critical thought, try to reframe it with a more compassionate response. Instead of telling yourself, "I'm a failure," you might say, "I had a setback, but that doesn't make me a failure. Everyone

experiences difficulties."

- **Write a personal letter to yourself:** Write a letter as if you were comforting a dear friend. What would you tell them? What words of encouragement or comfort would you offer? Now, read the letter to yourself and let those words sink in.
- **Practice self-care:** Regular exercise, a healthy diet, adequate sleep, and time for relaxation and recreation are all forms of self-care that express self-compassion. By taking care of your physical needs, you're also nurturing your emotional well-being.

Self-compassion isn't always easy, especially if you're accustomed to being hard on yourself. But remember, this is a journey, not a destination. And just like any other skill, self-compassion can be cultivated with patience and practice. Let's make a commitment to become a kind and compassionate friend to ourselves, as

# CHAPTER 37: ESTABLISHING EFFECTIVE ROUTINES

"Routine, in an intelligent man, is a sign of ambition." These wise words from the renowned writer W.H. Auden form the crux of our chapter today. As we venture further into our journey, let's stop for a moment and appreciate the hidden power of routines in our quest to ignite confidence, positivity, and motivation.

Have you ever observed the routine of a successful athlete or an accomplished musician? There's a method to the madness that constitutes their daily routines. Whether it's the exact time they wake up, the food they eat, or the particular way they practice their craft, these routine elements combine to create a powerful force that propels them toward success.

But why do routines matter? When we establish a routine, we create a consistent pattern in our lives that subconsciously begins to drive our actions. This predictability provides a sense of control and comfort, thereby reducing stress and enhancing our overall well-being.

Now, let's explore the steps to creating effective routines:

1. **Identify Your Priorities:** Your routine should revolve around your goals and priorities. Whether it's developing a fitness habit, dedicating time to self-reflection, or working on your personal projects, identify what's important to you and make it a part of

your daily routine.

2. **Start Small:** You don't need to overhaul your entire life in one go. Begin with one or two small changes and gradually add more as you become comfortable. A small victory, like waking up a half-hour earlier, can lay the foundation for larger success.

3. **Consistency is Key:** It's not what we do once in a while that shapes our lives, but what we do consistently. Make sure your new habit is performed regularly. It may be difficult initially, but with time, it'll become second nature.

4. **Be Flexible**: While routines provide a structure, rigidity can lead to burnout. Allow some flexibility. If you miss a step in your routine, don't stress. Remember, it's progress, not perfection, that matters.

5. **Review and Adjust:** Just as we grow and evolve, our routines should too. Regularly review your routine to ensure it still serves your goals and adjust as needed.

As we conclude this chapter, I invite you to embark on an experiment. Identify one habit you'd like to incorporate into your routine and follow the steps outlined above. Remember, change is a process. Be patient with yourself. It may seem challenging at first, but with persistence, you'll notice the power a simple routine can have in sparking your confidence, positivity, and motivation.

Tomorrow is a new day, a fresh start. So, let's welcome it with an effective routine that paves the way toward your goals and the realization of your potential.

"Your life today is essentially the sum of your habits." - James Clear. Let's make those habits count.

## Exercise: Adding a new habit

*Identify one habit you'd like to incorporate into your daily routine and make a plan to integrate it. Start small and be consistent. Remember, the journey of a thousand miles begins with a single step.*

# CHAPTER 38: ENHANCING FOCUS AND CONCENTRATION

Your mind is like a laser beam. When it's scattered, it's merely a source of light, but when focused, it has the power to cut through the toughest obstacles. In this chapter, we will be talking about enhancing your focus and concentration, the two core elements that directly fuel your productivity and success.

Most of us are quite familiar with the situation where we sit down to work on a task, only to find our minds wandering off after a few minutes. Whether it's our constantly buzzing phone, a distant conversation, or just our inner thoughts, it seems there's always something trying to steal away our attention. But remember, without focus, all the positivity, confidence, and motivation we've talked about in the previous chapters cannot be effectively put to use.

## Understanding Focus and Concentration

Focus is the ability to direct your attention towards a particular task while ignoring other distractions. On the other hand, concentration is the ability to maintain that focus over a certain period. They are the bedrock upon which all productive actions are built. In this digital age of constant distractions, improving focus and concentration has become more important than ever.

## The Role of Mindfulness in Focus

Mindfulness is a mental state where you are fully present in the moment, not thinking about the past or worrying about the future. Your mind is like a muscle, it can be trained and improved over time with practices like meditation. By practicing mindfulness, you're training your mind to focus on the present task, thereby enhancing your ability to concentrate.

## The Pomodoro Technique

One of the most popular methods to improve focus and concentration is the Pomodoro Technique. Named after a tomato-shaped kitchen timer, the method involves breaking your work into 25-minute intervals, known as "Pomodoros," each followed by a five-minute break. This technique works by tackling distraction and procrastination head-on, allowing you to maintain a high level of productivity for extended periods.

## Declutter Your Environment

Having a cluttered work environment can lead to a cluttered mind. Your physical environment can significantly impact your mental state, affecting your ability to focus. Aim for a clean, organized workspace, free from unnecessary distractions. This not only makes it easier for you to concentrate but also makes your tasks seem less daunting.

## Taking Care of Your Body

Physical health has an ongoing, profound impact on our mental capabilities. Adequate regular exercise, an intentional balanced diet, and adequate sleep can greatly enhance your ability to focus and concentrate. Physical activities stimulate the release of chemicals in the brain that help improve memory and cognitive functions.

## Final Words

In the end, improving focus and concentration isn't about forcing yourself to work relentlessly. It's about managing your energy, knowing when to take breaks, and setting up an environment conducive to focused work. It's about becoming the master of your own attention and directing it toward the tasks and goals that truly matter to you.

### Exercise: Practice Pomodoro

*As a small exercise, try the Pomodoro Technique tomorrow for your tasks. Note how your productivity changes and reflect on how you feel throughout the day. Additionally, try to incorporate 10 minutes of mindfulness practice into your daily routine and observe its impact on your focus over time.*

Remember, Rome wasn't built in a day. Just as you cannot expect to run a marathon without training, you cannot expect your focus and concentration to improve overnight. But with consistent effort, you will find your ability to concentrate getting better, allowing you to unleash the full power of your Spark.

# CHAPTER 39: HARNESSING THE POWER OF NOW

"The future is not yet here, and the past is already gone; all we truly have is the now." – Unknown.

This chapter of "Spark: Ignite Your Confidence, Positivity, and Motivation" is dedicated to an invaluable tool for building confidence and positivity: the power of now. We often find ourselves either trapped in the memories of our past or anxious about the uncertainty of the future. However, the secret to our confidence and motivation lies in embracing the present moment.

In recent years, mindfulness has gained considerable attention, and for a good reason. Mindfulness is the practice of bringing our attention to the present moment. This seemingly simple technique holds transformative power for our mental and emotional well-being. It improves our focus, reduces stress, and fosters emotional stability - all critical components of building confidence and maintaining motivation.

## Understanding the Power of Now

Mindfulness invites us to pay attention to the now, the present moment without judgment or interpretation. When we practice mindfulness, we're not thinking about what has happened or what might happen. Instead, we experience life as it unfolds, becoming keen observers of our thoughts, feelings, and actions.

## The Obstacles to Living in the Now

Despite the benefits, staying present isn't always easy. Our minds are designed to jump between past, present, and future. This jumping often leads to anxiety, regret, worry, and fear. Mind wandering, often viewed as harmless daydreaming, can rob us of our joy in the present moment.

## The Role of Mindfulness in Harnessing the Power of Now

Mindfulness helps us cultivate a non-judgmental awareness of the present moment. It trains our minds to focus on what's happening right now instead of dwelling on the past or worrying about the future.

## Practical Techniques for Harnessing the Power of Now

To help you cultivate the habit of living in the now, here are some techniques:

**Breathing exercises:** A few minutes of conscious breathing can help you bring your focus back to the present moment. Pay attention to the sensation of your breath coming in and going out.

**Body scan:** This involves bringing attention to different parts of your body, from your toes to the crown of your head. This helps ground you in the present moment.

**Mindful eating:** Pay attention to the tastes, textures, smells, and colors of your food. Eating mindfully can enhance your enjoyment and satisfaction.

**Observing nature:** Spend time in nature, taking in the sights, sounds, and smells. This practice can help you feel more connected to the present moment.

Remember, mindfulness is not about achieving a particular state or feeling; it's about being present with whatever arises, without judgment.

Harnessing the power of now can significantly boost your

confidence and motivation. The present moment is where life happens. By learning to stay present, you can fully engage with life, experiencing it in all its richness and complexity, thus igniting your confidence, positivity, and motivation.

Today, take a step to live more fully in the present. Harness the power of now and let your Spark ignite.

## Exercise: Mindfulness techniques

*Today, try to incorporate one of the mindfulness techniques into your daily routine. Observe any changes in your mood, focus, and overall sense of well-being.*

Remember, your journey is unique to you. Be gentle with yourself and take it one day at a time. The goal is to make steady progress, not to attain perfection.

# CHAPTER 40: EMPATHY: UNDERSTANDING OTHERS

The ability to see and feel the world through the eyes of another, to step into their shoes and understand their perspective, is the essence of empathy. Harnessing the power of empathy can lead to stronger, healthier relationships, an increased capacity for understanding, and a powerful boost to your confidence, positivity, and motivation. It's a fundamental ingredient in your quest to ignite your spark.

### Understanding Empathy

Empathy isn't just about feeling sorry for someone. It's a deeper, more profound emotion that involves understanding the feelings, thoughts, fears, anxieties, goals and emotions of others. Empathy is about recognizing the shared human experience and acknowledging the emotional states of others. It helps to bridge gaps and foster connections between individuals and groups, thus becoming a cornerstone for meaningful relationships.

Empathy doesn't come naturally to everyone, but like most skills, it can be cultivated and developed. Here, we delve into understanding the nature of empathy and how to tap into its power.

## Cultivating Empathy

**Active Listening**: Start by paying attention to others, actively listening to their words and the emotions behind them. It's not just about hearing but truly understanding the thoughts and feelings being expressed. The goal is to receive their perspective, devoid of your interpretations or judgments.

**Emotional Intelligence**: Emotional intelligence is a critical subset of our overall intelligence and is often defined as the capability/capacity to recognize, understand, and manage your emotions and those of others. As you grow in emotional intelligence, your capacity for empathy also increases, helping you connect better with others.

**Cultivate Curiosity:** Be genuinely curious about other people's experiences and viewpoints. Ask open-ended questions that prompt others to share more about their feelings and thoughts.

**Practice Perspective**-Taking: Deliberately try to see things from another's viewpoint. This shift in perspective helps you understand their emotions better and aids in building a connection.

## The Power of Empathy

Empathy plays a crucial role in personal and professional relationships. By showing understanding and compassion, you earn trust, respect, and appreciation. This, in turn, can improve your mental health by increasing your confidence, positivity, and motivation. When people feel seen and understood, they are more likely to reciprocate the same feelings, creating a virtuous cycle of positive relationships.

Empathy also expands your worldview, challenging your assumptions and fostering learning. It's a powerful tool that can help in conflict resolution, improve communication, and build team cohesion.

## Empathy in Action

As you journey towards cultivating empathy, be patient with yourself. It's not about being perfect but about making an honest attempt to understand others. Remember, empathy is not about losing yourself or your feelings; it's about recognizing and appreciating the emotions of others.

### Exercise: Someone else's shoes

*Think about someone close to you who is going through a challenging situation. Try to imagine what they might be feeling. Write down these feelings and thoughts.*

*Now, write a letter to them expressing your understanding and offering support. You don't have to send it; the goal here is to exercise your empathy muscles.*

Building empathy is a journey, not a destination. It takes practice and patience, but the rewards are well worth it. As you develop this skill, you'll find your connections with others deepening, your perspective broadening, and your inner spark growing brighter.

# CHAPTER 41: CREATING A VISION BOARD

Visualization is a powerful tool for nurturing your confidence, positivity, and motivation. It's one thing to imagine a future filled with success, fulfillment, and happiness. But it's another to represent these dreams and aspirations visually. That's where a vision board comes in. A vision board is more than just a collage of pretty pictures and inspirational quotes; it's a tangible representation of your future, a manifestation of your dreams.

Firstly, let's understand what a vision board is. Simply put, it's a visual display created to represent the future you desire. This could include images, phrases, quotes, or anything else that resonates with your aspirations. The board serves as a daily reminder and representation of your goals that you wish to achieve, motivating and inspiring you toward your success.

Now, the question arises: How do we create a compelling vision board? Here are some steps to guide you:

**1. Reflection:** Spend some time in quiet introspection. What do you want your future to look like? What are your goals in different aspects of life, like your career, relationships, health, personal growth, or leisure?

**2. Collection:** Begin collecting images, quotes, or objects that align with your dreams and aspirations. These could be cut-outs from magazines, printed photos, inspirational words, or even personal items that hold meaning for you.

**3. Assembly:** Now, it's time to bring everything together. Get a large piece of cardboard or poster board as your base. Arrange and affix your chosen items on the board in a way that appeals to you. There is no right or wrong way to do this; the board is a reflection of you and your dreams.

**4. Display**: Place your vision board somewhere you will see it every day. This could be your bedroom, study, or workspace. It should be in a place that allows you to engage with it regularly.

**5. Engagement:** Engage with your vision board daily. Spend a few moments each day looking at it, absorbing the images and their significance, allowing them to reinforce your goals and desires in your subconscious mind.

Creating a vision board is not about creating an artifact to be admired but about committing to a process of personal growth and actualization. Your vision board will evolve as you do, reflecting changes in your aspirations and circumstances.

Remember, the vision board is not a magical tool. It doesn't work by itself. It works by serving as a daily reminder of your dreams and aspirations, helping you to stay focused and motivated, encouraging positive thinking, and nurturing the belief that you can achieve what you set your mind to.

As you progress on your journey, don't forget to celebrate milestones, however small they may seem. Success is a journey, not a destination. Your vision board is a testament to this journey, a visual diary of your dreams and aspirations, and a constant reminder of the steps you are taking to realize them.

In the next chapter, we will delve into a different kind of hurdle you might face on your journey: self-sabotage. How can you identify it, and more importantly, how can you overcome it? Stay tuned as we continue this journey of self-discovery and growth.

# CHAPTER 42: IDENTIFYING AND OVERCOMING SELF-SABOTAGE

Have you ever found yourself on the brink of achieving something great, only to be stopped by a mysterious force that seems to come from within? This chapter is about that force - the force of self-sabotage.

Self-sabotage is the conscious or unconscious act of hindering one's own progress or goals. It is a complex phenomenon that can take many forms, such as procrastination, self-medication, or persistently maintaining negative relationships. Regardless of its form, self-sabotage is a widespread issue that can seriously hinder personal growth, confidence, positivity, and motivation.

To break the cycle of self-sabotage, we must first understand its roots. Often, self-sabotage is driven by underlying fears or beliefs that we may not even be aware of. These could include fear of failure, fear of success, or deeply ingrained beliefs of unworthiness. Some people subconsciously sabotage their own efforts because success feels uncomfortable or undeserved or because failure, while painful, is familiar and predictable.

Identifying self-sabotage can be challenging, but it's not impossible. Start by paying close attention to patterns in your behavior and the outcomes they lead to. Do you often procrastinate when facing a big task or important deadline?

Do you find reasons to avoid opportunities that could lead to personal growth or success? Do you maintain relationships that drain your energy or diminish your self-esteem? All of these can be signs of self-sabotage.

Once you've identified your patterns of self-sabotage, it's time to dig deeper. This is where self-reflection and honesty come in. Ask yourself: What fears or beliefs might be driving these behaviors? This step might be challenging and uncomfortable, but it's also essential. It's only by uncovering and confronting these underlying issues that we can hope to overcome self-sabotage.

Now comes the most critical part: replacing self-sabotaging behaviors with healthier, more productive ones. This process isn't easy, and it won't happen overnight. But with patience, persistence, and perhaps a bit of professional guidance, it's entirely achievable.

Start by setting small, manageable goals and hold yourself accountable for reaching them. Celebrate your successes, no matter how small they may seem. Practice self-compassion and try to remember that everyone makes mistakes. And finally, surround yourself with positive influences - people who will support and encourage your growth, not hinder it.

Remember, overcoming self-sabotage is a journey, not a destination. It's okay to take it one step at a time. The important thing is to keep moving forward, no matter how slowly. In time, you'll find yourself breaking free from self-sabotaging patterns and moving closer to your true potential.

### Exercise: Journal of self-sabotage

*In this case, the exercise is to keep a journal for one week. In it, jot down any actions or decisions that you believe may have been influenced by self-sabotage. Reflect on what fears or beliefs might be driving these behaviors and how you can address them. This will not only help you become more aware of your patterns of self-sabotage but also start you on the path to overcoming them.*

Remember, self-sabotage is a hurdle, not a roadblock. With awareness, honesty, and determination, you can overcome it and move closer to the confident, positive, and motivated life you're capable of living. You have the spark within you. Now it's time to let it shine.

# CHAPTER 43: LEVERAGING FAILURE AS FEEDBACK

The greatest deception that holds many of us back is the belief that failure is the end and that it somehow confirms our inadequacy. On the contrary, failure is one of the most valuable resources available on the journey of personal development. In this chapter, we will explore how to turn failures into feedback that fuels growth.

Firstly, we need to understand that failure is not the opposite of success but part of it. Often, the most successful individuals have faced repeated failures before they found success. Think of Thomas Edison's numerous failed attempts to invent the lightbulb or J.K. Rowling's numerous rejections before "Harry Potter" was finally published. Failure is often a sign that you are pushing your boundaries, challenging your status quo, and venturing outside of your comfort zone. And that is where growth happens.

Embracing this perspective allows us to remove the sting from failure and see it for what it is: an opportunity to learn. But how do we actually go about doing this?

Reframe your failure: The language we use to talk about our experiences shapes our perceptions. Instead of saying, "I failed," say, "I learned." This simple shift can profoundly change how you feel about the experience and opens you up to the lessons it has to offer.

Evaluate your process: Often, failure is a sign that something in your approach needs to be adjusted. Take a step back and objectively assess your strategies and actions. What could you have done differently? What did you overlook? Use this insight to refine your process.

Practice resilience: It's natural to feel disappointed or disheartened when things don't go as planned. But the ability to bounce back - resilience - is what separates those who ultimately succeed from those who do not. Practice self-compassion, give yourself time to recuperate, then rise again, armed with new knowledge and renewed determination.

Seek feedback from others: Don't just rely on your own perspective. Sometimes, others can provide valuable insights that we may miss. Reach out to mentors, peers, or even critics to gain a more comprehensive understanding of where things went wrong.

Implement changes: Use the feedback you've gathered to create an action plan for moving forward. This might involve learning new skills, changing your approach, or even questioning your goals. Implementation is crucial because, without it, the feedback is just information, not a tool for growth.

Remember, the path to success is often littered with failures. Each one is a checkpoint that brings you one step closer to your goal. Don't fear them, but learn from them. With each stumble, you are not falling away from your goal but taking a step forward in your understanding of how to get there.

To conclude this chapter, think about a recent failure in your life. Now, apply the steps mentioned above to that failure. What lessons can you extract from it? How can you use this feedback to alter your path to success? Reflect on this, and see how this changes your feelings towards failure.

# CHAPTER 44: MAXIMIZING ENERGY AND PERFORMANCE

What if you had a switch, which, once flipped, could unleash a wave of energy that helps you perform at your best every day? Although such a switch doesn't exist literally, the good news is that you can indeed maximize your energy and performance with the right strategies.

### Understanding Energy

Energy, unlike time, is renewable. How often have you heard the phrase, "I wish I had more time"? We can't add more hours to a day, but we can surely maximize our energy levels to make the most out of the hours we have. Energy is the vigor and vitality that gives you the strength to perform tasks and engage with the world around you. Understanding how your body and mind produce and use energy can help you leverage it effectively.

### The Energy Equation

Two fundamental elements influence your energy levels - physical well-being and mental health. Physical well-being relates to how well you treat your body. Are you eating right? Are you exercising regularly? Are you sleeping enough? Each of these contributes to your energy levels. On the other hand, mental health touches on your psychological and emotional well-being. Stress, anxiety, negative thoughts - all deplete your energy reserves, leaving you feeling drained.

## Fueling Your Body Right

What you eat impacts how you feel. Therefore, consuming a planned balanced diet, rich in fresh fruits, fresh vegetables, lean proteins, and whole grains, will provide sustained energy throughout the day. It's crucial to drink enough water as well since dehydration can cause fatigue. Avoid excessive intake of processed foods, sugary drinks, and caffeine, as these lead to energy crashes.

## Energize with Exercise

Regular physical activity is a powerful energy booster. It improves heart health, increases strength, and releases chemicals like endorphins in your brain that make you feel happier and more energized. Even a simple walk can do wonders to your energy levels.

## The Power of Sleep

Underestimating the power of a good night's sleep is one of the biggest mistakes people make. Sleep is the time when your body repairs itself, processes information, and recharges for the next day. A lack of sufficient sleep can result in a sluggish mind and a tired body.

## Mental Energy Boosters

Maintaining positive thoughts and managing stress effectively can boost your mental energy. Practices like meditation, yoga, and mindfulness can help in this regard. Surround yourself with positivity. Reading an inspiring book, listening to uplifting music, spending time with loved ones - all can replenish your mental energy.

## Pacing Your Energy

Pacing is crucial. The human body operates on ultradian

rhythms, cycles that last less than 24 hours. One of these is the 'energy cycle,' which ebbs and flows throughout the day. Understanding your energy cycle can help you schedule tasks better. High-energy periods are ideal for complex tasks, while low-energy periods are better suited for routine tasks.

### The Power of Breaks

Taking regular breaks can recharge your energy levels. The Pomodoro technique, where you work for a specific time (e.g., 25 minutes) and then take a short break (e.g., 5 minutes), has been effective for many.

### Energy and Performance: The Connection

Energy fuels performance. Higher energy levels help you concentrate better, make effective decisions, and stay motivated. Being energized doesn't just make you feel good; it enhances your productivity and overall performance.

### Action Points

This chapter isn't just about understanding how to maximize your energy and performance; it's about putting this knowledge into practice. Here are some action points:

- **Assess Your Diet**: Keep a food diary for a week. Note down what and when you eat and how you feel afterward. This will help you identify what works best for your body.
- **Start Exercising Regularly:** If you're not already, aim to incorporate a minimum of 30 minutes of moderate-intensity exercise into your daily routine. Find an activity you enjoy, be it dancing, swimming, or simply walking.
- **Improve Your Sleep Hygiene:** Ensure you're getting 7-9 hours of quality sleep each night. Maintain a consistent sleep schedule, create a restful environment, and establish a relaxing pre-sleep

routine.
- **Practice Stress Management Techniques**: Choose a method that resonates with you, be it meditation, deep breathing, yoga, or journaling. Aim to practice it regularly.
- **Understand Your Energy** Cycle: Keep a log for a week, noting down your energy levels at different times of the day. This will help you identify your peak energy times.
- **Take Regular Breaks**: Try using the Pomodoro technique or simply ensure that you step away from your work every hour or so to recharge.
- **Stay Hydrated:** Always drink plenty of water throughout each day in order to avoid dehydration. Dehydration leads to feelings of fatigue and also has a detrimental effect on your mental health as well.

Maximizing energy and performance is about aligning your lifestyle with your body's natural rhythms and looking after both your physical and mental health. When you feel energized, you can perform at your best and truly ignite the spark of confidence, positivity, and motivation within you.

In conclusion, remember this quote by Jim Loehr: "Energy, not time, is the fundamental currency of high performance." Embrace the strategies discussed in this chapter to boost your energy levels, and watch as your performance soars.

# CHAPTER 45: UNDERSTANDING THE POWER OF LANGUAGE

Language is the essence of expression. It's how we communicate our thoughts, feelings, and ideas to ourselves and others. More than solely being a medium of communication, our language shapes our perception of reality and influences our actions. As renowned cognitive scientist Steven Pinker once said, "Language is a window into human nature." This chapter explores the power of language and how it can impact your confidence, positivity, and motivation.

### The Impact of Language on Thoughts and Feelings

Language doesn't merely describe your reality; it defines it. The words you use can significantly affect how you interpret situations, how you feel about yourself, and how you interact with the world. When you describe a task as "difficult," you've already set a tone of struggle and hardship before even starting. But when you describe the same task as a "challenge," it implies a hurdle that can be overcome, influencing you to adopt a problem-solving approach.

### The Self-Fulfilling Prophecy of Words

Negative self-talk is a prime example of the power language

holds over us. Phrases like "I can't do it" or "I'm not good enough" can diminish self-esteem and hinder personal growth. On the flip side, positive self-talk such as "I can handle this" or "I'm doing my best" can boost confidence and motivation. This is not about unthinkingly ignoring the reality but about framing it in a way that empowers you.

### Language and Relationships

The language you use also impacts your relationships with others. Positive and respectful communication can build strong, harmonious relationships, while negative and disrespectful language can lead to misunderstandings and conflicts. The adage "It's not what you say, but how you say it" underscores the importance of not just the words but the tone of language.

### Transformative Power of Affirmations

Affirmations are positive statements that you say to yourself in order to combat negative thoughts and reinforce a belief in your capabilities. Regularly repeating affirmations can influence your subconscious mind, helping you cultivate a positive mindset and boosting your self-confidence.

### Action Points

Here are some practical steps you can take to harness the power of language:

- **Mind Your Self-Talk**: Monitor your internal dialogue. When you catch yourself using negative language, consciously reframe it in a positive or neutral way.
- **Use Empowering Language:** Choose words that instill confidence and motivation. Instead of saying, "I have to," say, "I get to." This slight shift can make tasks feel less like obligations and more like opportunities.
- **Practice Affirmations:** Develop a set of positive affirmations that resonate with you. Repeat them to yourself every morning or during challenging times to

reinforce positivity and confidence.

- **Communicate Positively:** Be mindful of the words you use when interacting with others. Practice active listening, show empathy, and respond with kindness and respect.
- **Language Learning:** If feasible, learn a new language. This not only enhances cognitive skills but also exposes you to different ways of thinking and expressing ideas.

Remember, language has power, and you have control over the language you use. By consciously choosing empowering language, you can influence your thoughts, shape your reality, and ignite your confidence, positivity, and motivation. So, as Robin Sharma wisely said, "Change your language, and you change your thoughts." Let your language be a tool to uplift you and others, spreading sparks of positivity wherever you go.

# CHAPTER 46: THE ROLE OF BODY LANGUAGE

As you continue on this journey toward sparking and nurturing your confidence, positivity, and motivation, it's vital to understand that communication isn't just about the words you say. It extends far beyond that, often deeply into non-verbal territory. This chapter aims to illustrate the power and significance of body language in projecting and shaping our confidence, positivity, and motivation.

Body language, or non-verbal communication, includes all the non-word-based communication methods we use daily. It includes facial expressions, gestures, posture, eye contact, touch, and even the space we maintain from others. Studies suggest that body language may constitute more than half of what we communicate to others, so its mastery is crucial in our journey.

As psychologist Amy Cuddy suggests in her popular TED Talk, our body language not only influences how others see us, but it can also change how we see ourselves. She advocates for the use of 'power posing'—which involves standing in a posture of confidence, even if we don't feel confident—to impact testosterone and cortisol levels within your brain which might also improve our chances for success.

This isn't about faking it until you make it but more about faking it until you become it. It's about harnessing the power of body language to shape your mind and emotions positively, boosting your self-belief and resilience in the process.

Let's explore some practical ways to use body language for our benefit.

- **Adopt a Confident Posture:** Stand or sit straight, pull your shoulders back, and lift your chin—this posture projects confidence and increases feelings of self-assuredness. Conversely, slumping or slouching can make you feel more insecure and less energetic.
- **Maintain Eye Contact:** Eye contact conveys attentiveness, interest, and presence, which can help you in both personal and professional interactions. However, be careful not to stare, as it can come off as aggressive or intrusive.
- **Smile More:** Smiling not only makes us appear friendly and approachable but can also trigger a release of mood-boosting hormones like endorphins. Moreover, it's often contagious, spreading positivity to others.
- **Use Open Gestures:** Open body language, like uncrossed arms or legs and gesturing with palms up, can show openness and honesty, making you more likable and trustworthy.
- **Mind Your Personal** Space: Respecting personal space can foster a sense of comfort and trust in interactions. Conversely, invading someone's personal space can cause discomfort or unease.

Remember, change does not happen overnight, and it takes practice to incorporate these aspects into your natural body language. Start with small steps, maybe by practicing a confident posture during your next meeting or maintaining eye contact during a conversation with a friend.

Body language, like any language, is a form of expression and understanding. It offers a window into our inner states, including confidence, positivity, and motivation. Learning to use it effectively can transform how we present ourselves to the world and how we perceive ourselves, creating a positive feedback loop that enhances our self-belief and self-efficacy.

Your journey is not merely about sparking the flame of confidence, positivity, and motivation but about fueling it consistently and effectively. And understanding the role of body language is a significant step in that direction.

In the next chapter, we will delve into the concept of self-image and how cultivating a positive self-image can serve as a powerful tool in your personal development toolkit.

# CHAPTER 47: CULTIVATING A POSITIVE SELF-IMAGE

A positive self-image is the psychological cornerstone of your confidence, positivity, and motivation. When we perceive ourselves positively, we feel good about who we are, appreciate our unique strengths, and foster a sense of worthiness. This chapter will explore the concept of self-image, why it's crucial to our well-being, and how we can cultivate a positive self-image.

Your self-image is like a mental portrait of yourself; it's how you see yourself based on your beliefs and experiences. This image is influenced by various factors, such as the feedback you receive from others, your successes and failures, and societal standards of success and beauty. A healthy self-image equips you with confidence and resilience, enabling you to approach life's challenges with a positive attitude.

However, it's important to understand that your self-image is subjective—it isn't an exact reflection of reality but rather a perception influenced by your thoughts and experiences. This subjective nature of self-image is empowering because it means you have the capacity to change it.

To cultivate a positive self-image, the first step is to become aware of how you see yourself. Awareness breeds control, and it's only when you're aware of your self-perceptions that you can start to change them. Reflect on your self-talk—what you say to yourself about yourself. If it's predominantly negative, work on shifting to more positive, affirming language.

## Exercise: Counteracting negativity

*Write down a list of five things you frequently say or think about yourself that are negative or limiting. Next to each, write a positive, empowering statement that counteracts the negative one. For instance, if one negative statement is "I'm not good at public speaking," you might counteract it with, "I am capable of learning and improving my public speaking skills."*

Another critical aspect of cultivating a positive self-image is focusing on your strengths rather than your weaknesses. It's easy to zero in on what we perceive as flaws and overlook our skills and abilities. Instead of berating yourself for what you're not good at, take time each day to acknowledge and appreciate your strengths. Write down what you're good at, what you like about yourself, and your achievements, no matter how small.

Remember that everyone has strengths and weaknesses. Just because you're not good at something doesn't mean you're not good at anything. Be fair and balanced in your self-assessment, recognizing both your successes and areas for improvement.

Finally, take care of your physical health. Regular intentional exercise, a balanced diet, and adequate rest can boost your self-image. When you feel good physically, it positively impacts your mental and emotional state, reinforcing a positive self-image.

Cultivating a positive self-image is a process. There will be good days and challenging ones, but each step, each positive thought about yourself, each acknowledgment of your strengths brings you closer to seeing yourself in a more positive light.

Remember, your self-image is not set in stone; it's more like a painting that evolves over time. With each brushstroke of positive self-perception and self-appreciation, you create a masterpiece of confidence, positivity, and motivation.

In the next chapter, we will explore how a positive self-image can empower you to make decisions confidently.

# CHAPTER 48: MAKING DECISIONS WITH CONFIDENCE

As you journey through the chapters of this book, you've been learning about confidence, positivity, and motivation. Now, it's time to home in on an integral part of life, one that can elicit fear and anxiety but equally provide a sense of accomplishment and growth - the act of making decisions. Specifically, we will delve into making decisions with confidence.

At the heart of every decision is a crossroad. Each path leading away from this junction represents a different outcome, and it is natural to feel uneasy about which direction to take. But remember, indecision is a decision in itself - one that often leads to stagnation. The key is not to avoid decision-making but to approach it with confidence.

### Knowledge is Power

Decision-making is less daunting when you're armed with knowledge. Educate yourself about the decision at hand. Gather facts, consider the possibilities, and make sure you're making an informed choice. The more information you have, the more confident you will be in your decision.

### Embrace the Uncertainty

No decision comes with a 100% guarantee of success. Embrace the uncertainty that comes with decision-making. Remember that every decision, good or bad, is an opportunity to learn and grow.

### Trust Your Intuition

Sometimes, the best decisions are made when we listen to our intuition. Our subconscious mind has a way of piecing together information faster than our conscious mind. It's that gut feeling or instinct that speaks to us. While it's crucial to make informed decisions, don't discount your intuition.

### Avoid Paralysis by Analysis

Overanalyzing can lead to decision paralysis. At some point, you need to take a leap of faith and make the decision. Not every decision will be perfect, and that's okay. It's more important to make a decision and adjust as necessary than to remain stuck in analysis.

### Learn from the Past, but Don't Be Hindered by It

Past decisions, especially those that didn't pan out as hoped, can make us hesitant. But don't let past failures undermine your decision-making confidence. Instead, treat them as learning opportunities to make better decisions in the future.

### Consult Others, But Own Your Decision

It can often be helpful to search out advice from others, especially those who have been in similar situations or whose opinions you value. However, the final decision must be yours. Own your decision and be responsible for its outcome.

In the end, confidence in decision-making comes from accepting that not all decisions will lead to the expected outcome. It's about understanding that making a 'wrong' decision doesn't make you a failure, and being stuck in indecision can be more detrimental than making an incorrect decision. Remember, every decision is an opportunity for growth, and with each decision made, your confidence will grow.

## Exercise – Decision Making

*To practice making decisions with confidence, write down a decision you've been struggling with. List the pros and cons, consult others if needed, and trust your intuition. Then make the decision, own it, and see it through, ready to learn from whatever the outcome may be.*

# CHAPTER 49: CULTIVATING A WINNING ATTITUDE

A winning attitude. We've all heard the phrase. But what does it truly mean? And, more importantly, how can we cultivate it?

A winning attitude doesn't necessarily mean always being the first or the best. It's not about never experiencing failure or setbacks. On the contrary, a winning attitude is about embracing every part of the journey, with its ups and downs, as an opportunity to learn, grow, and improve. It's about seeing obstacles as stepping stones rather than roadblocks. It's about recognizing that real success lies not in the end goal but in the resilience, perseverance, and growth that come from striving for it.

This chapter will explore the components of a winning attitude, the benefits it can bring to your life, and how you can cultivate it.

## Embrace Growth and Learning

A winning attitude starts with a growth mindset, which we've covered in Chapter 4. It's about understanding that skills and abilities can be developed and seeing every experience as an opportunity to learn. When you make a mistake or face a setback, don't view it as a failure. Instead, ask yourself: "What can I learn from this?"

## Practice Optimism

Optimism is a key element of a winning attitude. It's about expecting the best possible outcome and seeing the positive aspects of any situation without ignoring or denying its challenges. Optimism doesn't mean ignoring reality; it means believing in your ability to handle that reality and turn it to your advantage.

### Be Persistent

A winning attitude requires persistence. It's about having the determination to keep going, even when the going gets tough. It's about understanding that success is not a straight line and that it often comes to those who simply refuse to give up. When faced with a challenge, remind yourself: "I can do this. I will keep going."

### Cultivate Resilience

Resilience is all about the individual ability to bounce back from setbacks and difficulties. It's about being able to withstand stress and adversity and come out stronger on the other side. Developing resilience is crucial to cultivating a winning attitude because it helps you navigate the inevitable ups and downs of life with grace and fortitude.

### Focus on the Journey, and the Joy that Brings, Not Just the Destination

Finally, a winning attitude means focusing on the journey, not just the destination. It's about finding joy and fulfillment in the process of striving for your goals, not just in achieving them. It's about recognizing that success is not a destination but a journey of constant learning, growth, and improvement.

To cultivate a winning attitude:

- **Practice self-compassion**. Remember, nobody is perfect. Treat yourself with the same compassionate, caring, kindness and understanding attitide that you would give to a friend.

- **Set clear, achievable goals.** Having a defined sense of purpose and clear direction can motivate you to persevere in the face of challenges.
- **Surround yourself with positive influences.** The mindset of the people you spend time with can greatly influence your mindset. Surround yourself with those who lift you up and inspire you to be your best.
- **Adopt healthy lifestyle habits.** Adopting regular exercise, eating a balanced diet, and ensuring you have adequate sleep can boost your mood, energy, and overall outlook.
- **Practice mindfulness and gratitude.** These practices can help you stay focused on the present moment and appreciate the good in your life, boosting your optimism and resilience.

Remember, cultivating a winning attitude is a lifelong journey. It's not about being perfect; it's about striving to be the best you can be, learning and growing from every experience, and finding joy and fulfillment in the journey. With persistence, optimism, resilience, a focus on the journey, and a love for learning and growth, you can cultivate a winning attitude that will help you navigate life with confidence, positivity, and motivation.

# CHAPTER 50: THE POWER OF PATIENCE

The art of patience might seem out of place in a fast-paced, instant-gratification world. Yet, it's essential to igniting your confidence, positivity, and motivation. In this chapter, we'll uncover the true power of patience, not as passive waiting but as an active and rewarding endeavor in itself.

In a world where everyone seems to be racing to the finish line, we tend to undervalue the process of getting there. We become so focused on results that we forget to appreciate the journey. This is where patience plays a crucial role. It's about understanding that great things take time and learning to love the process of becoming.

Patience allows us to experience and learn from the journey, not just rush toward the destination. It is a characteristic of confidence, the manifestation of self-belief. A confident person knows that even if things do not happen right away, they will eventually if the effort and dedication are there.

Patience doesn't mean just waiting; it means maintaining a positive attitude and continuing to do your best, even when things don't go as planned. This perspective allows you to learn from setbacks rather than become discouraged by them. Patience is the antidote to frustration, the calm in the face of delay. It is the quiet confidence that things will unfold as they should, in their own time.

Now, it's time to dive into practical tips to cultivate patience in our lives:

- **Practice Mindfulness**: Being in the present moment allows you to appreciate what's happening now, reducing the urge for quick results. This can be done through meditation or simply taking a moment to breathe and observe your surroundings.
- **Set Realistic Expectations:** Remember that most worthwhile achievements take time. By setting realistic expectations, you allow yourself the time and space necessary to reach your goals.
- **Be Kind to Yourself:** Being impatient often results from being overly critical of oneself. Practice self-compassion, understanding that everyone, including you, is a work in progress.
- **See Obstacles as Opportunities:** Every delay or setback is an opportunity to learn and grow. Use these times to develop resilience and a deeper understanding of your journey.
- **Surround Yourself with Patience:** Spend time with patient people. Their calmness, resilience, and perspective can be infectious.
- **Patience Journal:** Keep a journal where you record instances where you've successfully exercised patience or when you could have been more patient. This can provide insight into patterns and trigger situations, guiding you on where to focus your efforts.

Patience isn't just a virtue; it's a skill that can be honed with practice. When you embrace patience, you'll find that you're not only more confident and motivated, but you're also better equipped to face life's challenges with a positive attitude. Remember, the journey to becoming your best self is a marathon, not a sprint. By cultivating patience, you'll find joy and growth in the journey itself, and before you know it, you'll have arrived at your desired destination.

# CHAPTER 51: RECOGNIZING AND COMBATTING NEGATIVITY BIAS

As humans, we have a predisposition to notice the bad more than the good. Psychologists refer to this phenomenon as negativity bias. But why do we do this, and how can we flip the script to support our journey toward confidence, positivity, and motivation? This chapter aims to help you identify, understand, and combat negativity bias.

First, let's delve into why negativity bias exists. Psychologists believe it's a product of evolution. Our ancestors had to be more attuned to potential dangers than to positive aspects of their environment to survive. While this hardwired sensitivity to negativity served a critical function in our evolutionary history, it can hinder us in our contemporary lives.

Negativity bias manifests in various ways. For instance, you may dwell more on a criticism than a compliment or anticipate the worst outcomes in a situation. Even a small negative incident can ruin an otherwise good day. But understanding negativity bias is the first step to overcoming it.

Here are some strategies to combat negativity bias:

- **Awareness:** The first step to addressing negativity bias is recognizing it. Monitor your thoughts and feelings throughout the day, acknowledging when you're focusing on negative aspects of a situation.

- **Mindfulness:** Mindfulness is the practice of being wholly present and accepting the current moment without judgment. When you notice negativity arising, practice mindfulness to accept these feelings without allowing them to consume you.
- **Gratitude:** Cultivating gratitude can shift your focus from negative aspects to positive ones. Make it a daily practice to identify things for which you're grateful.
- **Positivity Practice:** Make an effort to recognize and celebrate the good things happening around you. Take time each day to savor positive experiences, no matter how small they might seem.
- **Reframing:** When you catch yourself in negative thinking, try to reframe the situation. What can you learn from this experience? Is there a silver lining?
- **Self-Compassion**: Be kind to yourself when you notice negativity bias creeping in. Remember, it's a natural human tendency. Offer yourself compassion and understanding, as you would do for a friend.

Negativity bias is powerful, but it doesn't have to control your life. By recognizing and understanding this bias, you can implement strategies to combat it. These tools are not about denying or ignoring the negative aspects of life but about giving equal weight to the positive ones. So, keep practicing, and over time, you'll shift your mental landscape towards a more balanced, positive outlook. You will not only spark but fuel your confidence, positivity, and motivation on your journey to the life you want to lead.

# CHAPTER 52: MASTERING THE ART OF LISTENING

In a world of constant chatter and digital distractions, truly listening to others has become an underrated skill. Yet, it's this ability to be present and genuinely absorb what others say that fosters deeper connections, mutual understanding, and an enriched perspective on life. This chapter focuses on the art of listening and its role in boosting your confidence, positivity, and motivation.

Listening is about more than merely hearing words—it involves understanding, interpreting, and evaluating what you hear. It allows us to connect with others on a profound level and is a hallmark of strong, effective communication.

Here are some strategies to enhance your listening skills:

- **Be Present: Fully focus on the person speaking.** Try to block out your surroundings and silence your thoughts. Show that you're engaged with appropriate body language, such as maintaining eye contact and nodding when you understand.
- **Empathize: Put yourself in the speaker's shoes**. Try to understand their perspective and emotions. This empathy shows respect and makes people feel heard and understood.
- **Don't Interrupt:** Allow the speaker to finish their thought before you respond. Interruptions can disrupt

their flow of thought and may convey a lack of respect or interest.

- **Ask Open-Ended Questions:** To show your engagement and to understand the speaker's perspective better, ask questions that prompt more than a yes/no answer. This will encourage them to open up further and provide more detail.
- **Reflect and Validate:** Repeat what you've heard in your own words to confirm your understanding. Validating the speaker's feelings, even if you don't agree with their perspective, makes them feel heard and appreciated.
- **Avoid Judgement:** Keep an open mind when listening. Immediate criticism or disagreement can shut down open communication. Try to understand before being understood.
- **Listen to Non-Verbal Cues:** Communication is more than just words. Pay attention to the speaker's body language, tone, and facial expressions for a more complete understanding.

By mastering the art of listening, you create a nurturing environment for your relationships to thrive. It shows your respect for others, enhances your understanding of different perspectives, and allows you to learn from every conversation. Not only does it improve your interpersonal relationships, but it also makes you a more confident communicator.

Remember, active listening is a skill, and like any other skill, it requires practice. Begin by implementing these tips in your daily interactions and observe the positive changes that arise. In the grand journey to ignite your confidence, positivity, and motivation, the art of listening plays a fundamental role. It helps you connect with others and yourself on a deeper level, opening doors to richer experiences and stronger relationships. It's time to master this art and witness the spark it ignites in your life.

# CHAPTER 53: KEEPING COMMITMENTS TO YOURSELF

Have you ever made a promise to yourself, only to break it later? Perhaps you've vowed to eat healthier, go to bed earlier, or exercise daily but found yourself slipping back into old habits after a few days or weeks. If this resonates with you, you're not alone. Keeping commitments to oneself is often more challenging than fulfilling commitments to others. However, it's a vital skill to master on your journey to ignite your confidence, positivity, and motivation.

When you keep promises to yourself, you build self-trust. This trust is the foundation of self-confidence, and without it, any attempts to build your confidence, positivity, and motivation may be hindered. In contrast, every time you break a promise to yourself, you undermine your own trust and confidence. The impact may be subtle, but it's real and significant.

Here's how to start keeping your commitments to yourself:

- **Be Realistic:** Set commitments that are challenging yet achievable. Ensure they align with your current resources, capabilities, and lifestyle.
- **Start Small:** It's okay to start with small commitments, like waking up ten minutes earlier or drinking an extra glass of water a day. As your self-trust grows, you can take on bigger commitments.
- **Be Specific:** Clearly define what your commitment

entails. Instead of saying, "I will eat healthier," say, "I will eat at least five servings of fruit and vegetables every single day."

- **Write It Down:** The act of writing your commitment can make it feel more concrete and harder to ignore or forget. Keep it in a place where you can see it regularly.
- **Commit Publicly:** If you're comfortable, share your commitment with someone you trust. This creates accountability and can motivate you to stick to your commitment.
- **Reflect and Adjust:** If you struggle to keep a commitment, reflect on why this might be the case. Perhaps the commitment was too ambitious, or perhaps it's not as important to you as you initially thought. Adjust as necessary.
- **Celebrate Wins:** Each time you keep a commitment, celebrate it. This doesn't mean indulging in counterproductive rewards; instead, take a moment to acknowledge your achievement and feel proud.

Keeping commitments to yourself is like flexing a muscle—the more you do it, the stronger you become. It may seem challenging at first, but over time, it will become second nature. Remember, the goal is not to be perfect but to be consistent. Every now and then, you may slip, and that's okay. It's part of being human. The key is to acknowledge it, learn from it, and continue moving forward.

By cultivating the habit of keeping commitments to yourself, you lay a strong foundation for self-trust and self-confidence. You'll find that as you become more reliable to yourself, your self-confidence, positivity, and motivation will ignite and grow. As you journey towards a brighter, more positive, and more motivated self, remember that each commitment kept is another spark added to your growing flame.

# CHAPTER 54: THE IMPACT OF ALTRUISM

In our journey through this book, we have already explored the power of self-belief, resilience, gratitude, empathy, and so much more. Now, we shift our focus outwards to delve into an aspect that may seem to involve others more than ourselves - altruism. However, as we'll soon discover, engaging in altruistic behaviors has profound impacts on our own confidence, positivity, and motivation.

Altruism is the enactment of selfless concern for the health and welfare of others. It's about taking actions that benefit others without any expectation of reciprocation. This could be something as simple as helping an elderly neighbor with their groceries or as complex as devoting your time and resources to a humanitarian cause.

When you act altruistically, you send a powerful message to your subconscious mind: you have value to add to the world. This reinforces your self-worth and confidence. Additionally, altruism tends to evoke a sense of positivity, happiness, and satisfaction, often referred to as the "helper's high." This joy comes from knowing that you've made a difference in someone else's life, however small it may be.

Here are some ways to incorporate altruism into your daily life:

- **Volunteer:** Consider donating your time to a cause that resonates with you. This could be a local charity, a community project, or a global initiative.
- **Random Acts of Kindness:** Incorporate small, random

acts of kindness into your daily routine. These could include things like helping a stranger carry a heavy load, paying for someone's coffee, or leaving a positive note for someone to find.

- **Donate:** If you have the means, consider making a monetary donation to a charity you believe in. This could also be in the form of donating goods to those in need.
- **Be There for Others:** Sometimes, being altruistic simply means lending a listening ear to someone who needs it. Offering your time and attention can be a powerful act of kindness.
- **Share Knowledge and Skills:** If you have a particular skill or knowledge, consider sharing it with others. This could be in the form of tutoring, mentoring, or even sharing helpful resources online.

When practicing altruism, remember that it should never feel like a burden or an obligation. Instead, view it as an opportunity to enrich your own life as well as others. And remember, you don't have to make grand gestures for your actions to count. Even the tiniest acts of kindness can have a significant impact.

As you incorporate more altruistic behaviors into your life, you'll likely notice a boost in your overall mood and outlook on life. You'll feel more connected to the world around you and gain a deeper understanding of the positive impact you can have on others. This will not only fuel your motivation, but it will also stoke the fire of your confidence and positivity, helping your inner spark shine brighter than ever before.

# CHAPTER 55: BUILDING CONFIDENCE THROUGH COMPETENCE

When we think of confidence, we often think of it as an independent trait, something that some people are naturally endowed with. However, confidence does not exist in a vacuum. One of the strongest foundations upon which it is built is competence. Simply put, the more competent or skilled you are at something, the more confident you will feel doing it.

Competence is a measure of your ability to do something effectively and efficiently. It comes from knowledge, skills, experience, and the successful application of all three. It's like a cycle - you start with learning, which leads to skill acquisition, which, when applied successfully, builds competence, which in turn boosts your confidence.

Here's how you can build your confidence through competence:

- **Identify Your Strengths and Areas of Interest:** Begin by acknowledging what you're already good at. Maybe you're a great listener, a meticulous organizer, or a creative thinker. Similarly, recognize your areas of interest. Where do your passions lie? When you enjoy doing something, the likelihood of becoming competent at it increases substantially.

- **Set Learning Goals:** Once you've identified your strengths and interests, set specific, measurable, attainable, relevant, and time-bound (SMART) learning goals. This could be anything from learning a new language, mastering a software tool, or developing better communication skills.
- **Invest in Skill Acquisition:** Dedicate time and energy towards learning and improving your skills. Use resources like books, online courses, webinars, workshops, and more. Don't forget about the power of practice – it's key to moving from understanding to proficiency.
- **Seek Feedback and Learn From It:** Constructive feedback is a powerful tool for growth. Seek it out and view it as a means to improve, not as criticism. Remember, it's not a judgment of your worth but an opportunity to learn and grow.
- **Apply Your Skills:** As you learn, look for opportunities to apply your skills. This could be at work, in your personal life, or even in volunteer opportunities. Real-world application cements learning and builds competence.
- **Celebrate Your Progress:** Each step you take towards competence is a victory. Celebrate it. Recognizing and rewarding yourself for progress, however small, fuels motivation and builds your confidence.

Remember, confidence is not about knowing everything or being perfect. It's about trusting in your ability to learn, grow, and adapt. Building confidence through competence is a journey, not a destination. As you continue to learn and grow, your confidence will too. So, step out, take charge of your learning, and let your growing competence ignite the spark of confidence within you.

# CHAPTER 56: SEEKING AND GIVING CONSTRUCTIVE FEEDBACK

Feedback is an integral part of personal growth. It serves as a mirror that reflects our strengths and areas for improvement. Being open to feedback and understanding how to use it constructively can significantly accelerate your journey toward increased confidence, positivity, and motivation.

Part of this process is learning to seek out feedback actively and not just wait for it to come to you. Reaching out for feedback communicates a desire for growth and a willingness to take ownership of your development.

Here are some strategies for effectively seeking and giving constructive feedback:

Seeking Feedback:

- **Be Specific:** Instead of asking for general feedback, ask about specific instances or areas you're interested in improving. The more specific your request, the more targeted and useful the feedback will be.
- **Choose the Right People:** Look for feedback from those who have a good understanding of the area you want to improve in. They might be colleagues, mentors, coaches, or friends.

- **Be Open and Receptive:** When receiving feedback, listen actively and resist the urge to defend yourself. Remember, feedback is not personal criticism but an opportunity to learn and grow.
- **Reflect and Apply:** Once you've received feedback, take time to reflect on it. What steps can you take to improve based on the feedback? Create a plan of action and put it into practice.

Giving Feedback:

- **Be Constructive, Not Destructive:** Constructive feedback aims to build up, not tear down. It should be focused on actions or behaviors, not on the person. For example, instead of saying, "You're disorganized", you could say, "I noticed the report was a bit disorganized."
- **Be Specific and Clear:** Vague feedback is hard to act on. Be specific about what the person did well and where they can improve. Use clear and simple language to convey your point.
- **Focus on the Future:** Constructive feedback is forward-looking. Instead of dwelling on past mistakes, use them as a basis for future improvement. Offer practical suggestions or strategies for change.
- **Be Empathetic:** Put yourself in the other person's shoes. How would you want to receive feedback? Keep your tone and body language respectful and understanding.

Learning to seek and give feedback effectively takes time and practice, but it's a skill worth cultivating. Remember, feedback is a gift - one that offers insights for improvement and opens doors to becoming the best version of yourself. Embrace feedback, give it generously and kindly, and watch your confidence, positivity, and motivation soar.

# CHAPTER 57: OVERCOMING IMPOSTER SYNDROME

Imposter Syndrome is a psychological phenomenon where individuals doubt their accomplishments and harbor persistent internalized fear of being exposed as a "fraud." Despite whatever external evidence is provided of their competence, the individual remains convinced that they are imposters and do not deserve the success they have achieved.

Imposter Syndrome can be a significant roadblock on your journey toward increased confidence, positivity, and motivation. However, recognizing and overcoming it can propel you forward, allowing you to embrace your accomplishments and abilities fully.

Here are some strategies for dealing with Imposter Syndrome:

- **Recognize the Imposter Feelings:** Acknowledging these feelings when they arise is the first step to overcoming Imposter Syndrome. Pay attention to the self-talk that accompanies these feelings. Are they rational? Are they based on objective facts?
- **Talk About It:** Speaking about your feelings can often minimize their impact. You'd be surprised to find that many people, even highly successful individuals,

experience the same feelings. You're not alone in this, and sharing can help alleviate your worries.

- **Reframe Failure:** Changing your perspective on failure and mistakes is vital. They're not evidence of fraudulence but an integral part of growth and learning. See them as opportunities to learn and improve.
- **Embrace and Own Your Success**: Acknowledge your achievements and understand that they didn't occur by mere luck or accident but because of your skills, strengths, and perseverance. Celebrate your successes, no matter how small they might seem.
- **Seek and Accept Feedback:** As we discussed in the previous chapter, constructive feedback is a powerful tool for personal growth. It provides an objective assessment of your work and can help counteract feelings of being a fraud.
- **Practice Self-Compassion:** Be kind to yourself when you experience doubt or make mistakes. Self-criticism can fuel Imposter Syndrome, whereas self-compassion can extinguish it.

Imposter Syndrome can be a challenging adversary, but it's one that you can overcome. By applying these strategies, you can gradually chip away at the self-doubt and begin to see your accomplishments for what they truly are – a testament to your abilities, hard work, and dedication. Remember, everyone, experiences doubt, but don't let that doubt cloud the reality of your abilities and achievements. Keep your spark ignited, continue to strive for growth, and never let the imposter within you overshadow your shine.

# CHAPTER 58: EXPLORING MINDFULNESS AND MEDITATION

Mindfulness and meditation, though often used interchangeably, represent two distinct but interconnected practices. Mindfulness is the focused awareness that comes from paying specific attention, on purpose, in the present moment, and non-judgmentally. Meditation is a deliberative practice where an individual utilises techniques – such as mindfulness or focusing the mind onto a specific actual object, thought, or activity – in order to direct and focus attention and awareness and bring about a mentally clear and emotionally controlled, and stable state.

These practices have been shown to significantly improve mental clarity, emotional health, and overall well-being. When incorporated into your daily life, they can assist with reducing stress, increasing focus, and boosting your confidence, positivity, and motivation.

Here's how you can explore mindfulness and meditation:

- **Start Simple:** Begin by setting aside just a few minutes each day for mindfulness or meditation. You can gradually increase this time as your comfort with the practice grows.

- **Choose a Comfortable Space:** Your environment can significantly impact your ability to focus and relax. Choose a quiet, comfortable space where you won't be easily disturbed.
- **Focus on Your Breath:** A common technique for both mindfulness and meditation is focusing on your breath. Pay attention to the sensation of the air entering and leaving your body. This simple act can help ground you in the present moment.
- **Acknowledge Your Thoughts:** During meditation, you might find your mind wandering. That's okay! The aim isn't to eliminate thoughts but to acknowledge them without judgment and gently guide your attention back to your breath or another focus point.
- **Practice Mindfulness in Daily Activities:** Mindfulness can be practiced anytime, anywhere. Whether you're eating, walking, or simply sitting, pay attention to your senses and the world around you.
- **Use Guided Meditations:** If you're finding it hard to meditate on your own, guided meditations can be an excellent resource. They offer step-by-step instructions and can help you stay focused.
- **Keep a Journal:** Keeping a mindfulness or meditation journal which will assist you in tracking your progress and explore your thoughts and feelings more deeply.

Be Patient with Yourself: Just like any other skill, mindfulness and meditation require practice. If you find it challenging, don't beat yourself up. Remember, the journey is what's important.

Integrating mindfulness and meditation into your life might seem challenging at first, but with time, you'll likely find that they become a treasured part of your routine. As your ability to stay present and focused improves, so too will your confidence, positivity, and motivation. These practices not only help you find peace within yourself but also allow you to connect with the world around you in a more meaningful and enriching way.

By exploring mindfulness and meditation, you're fanning the flames of your spark, allowing it to shine brighter than ever before.

# CHAPTER 59: BUILDING EMOTIONAL RESILIENCE

Emotional resilience is the ability / capability to bounce back from adversity, trauma, and stress. It involves using different techniques and strategies to cope with, adapt to, and recover from challenging life events. This ability is like a muscle; with conscious effort and training, it can be developed, strengthened, and honed. The goal of this chapter is to guide you in building your emotional resilience, making you better equipped to handle life's challenges and bounce back from setbacks with even greater vigor.

## Understanding Emotional Resilience

Emotional resilience is not about avoiding difficulties or maintaining an artificial sense of positivity. It is about embracing the full range of human emotions and allowing ourselves to experience pain, loss, and failure without being overwhelmed by them. Resilient people feel the depth of emotion but also know how to recover from these situations and move forward.

## Recognize Your Emotions

Emotional resilience starts with recognizing our emotions and acknowledging their presence without judgment. By becoming aware of what we're feeling, we're better equipped to handle those emotions appropriately. Mindfulness, which we discussed in Chapter 58, is an effective way to enhance our emotional awareness.

## Practice Emotional Regulation

Once we've identified our emotions, we can then work on regulating them. Regulation techniques include such things as deep breathing, progressive muscle relaxation, and cognitive reframing. Remember, the goal is not to suppress or deny our feelings but to manage and respond to them in a healthy and adaptive manner.

## Build a Strong Support Network

Support from friends, family, and community plays a vital role in building emotional resilience. Having people to turn to when times are tough can provide us with a sense of belonging and help us navigate through life's storms.

## Develop a Growth Mindset

As discussed in Chapter 4, a growth mindset embraces challenges as opportunities for learning and growth. When we view setbacks as temporary and necessary for personal development, we build resilience and are better equipped to bounce back from adversity.

## Take Care of Your Physical Health

Our emotional health is intrinsically tied to our physical well-being. Regular focused exercise, an intentional balanced diet, and sufficient sleep can enhance our mood, reduce anxiety and depression, and increase our resilience to stress.

## Cultivate Gratitude

Gratitude, which we explored in Chapter 16, is a powerful tool for resilience. By focusing on the positive aspects of life, even during challenging times, we can foster resilience and enhance our overall well-being.

The journey to building emotional resilience is not linear, and it's okay to have days where you feel less resilient than others. Remember, resilience is built over time, and every step you take towards developing it, no matter how small, is a step in the right direction.

## Exercise: Resilience Plan

*Write down three situations where you showed resilience in the past. Reflect on what helped you overcome these challenges and bounce back. Use these insights to create a personal "Resilience Plan" that you can turn to when facing adversity in the future.*

Resilience is all about learning to dance in the rain whilst waiting for the storm to pass. By building your emotional resilience, you'll not only be able to weather life's storms but also to dance joyfully in the midst of them. So, let's embrace the challenge and start building your emotional resilience today!

# CHAPTER 60: ACCEPTING COMPLIMENTS GRACIOUSLY

"Thank you."

Two simple words that can sometimes be surprisingly difficult to say. Especially when they're in response to a compliment. In this chapter, we delve into the importance of accepting compliments graciously and how it ties into our self-confidence, positivity, and motivation.

The act of accepting compliments isn't just about politeness. It's a key element of self-confidence. When we downplay or dismiss a compliment, we're telling ourselves that we're not worthy of praise. This can be detrimental to our self-image and can hinder our personal growth.

Many of us struggle with accepting compliments because we fear coming off as arrogant or we simply don't believe we deserve them. But consider this: compliments are gifts of words from others. Just as you wouldn't dismiss or reject a physical gift, you shouldn't disregard the gift of praise.

Here's how to embrace compliments and use them to fuel your journey toward greater confidence, positivity, and motivation:

- **Simply Say 'Thank You':** The first step to accepting a compliment graciously is to say 'thank you.' It might feel uncomfortable at first, especially if you're used to deflecting compliments, but practice will make it feel more natural.

- **Believe in the Compliment**: When someone gives you a compliment, they're not just making an empty comment. They see something in you that they appreciate. Embrace it. Internalize it. Let it remind you of your strengths.
- **Avoid Deflecting**: It's easy to dismiss compliments by saying, "It was nothing" or "I was just lucky." Avoid this. Instead, acknowledge the effort or skill it took to achieve what you're being complimented on. It's okay to be proud of your achievements.
- **Reciprocate When Genuine:** If the compliment sparks a genuine admiration you have for the other person, it's a good moment to express it. It's not a requirement, but it can further positive interactions.
- **Use it as Fuel:** Compliments can be a wonderful source of motivation. They remind you of your abilities and can inspire you to continue striving towards your goals. Next time you receive a compliment, instead of brushing it off, use it as fuel to keep going.

## Exercise: Accepting compliments

*For the next week, consciously practice accepting compliments. Whether it's about your work, your appearance, or your actions - simply say thank you and let the words sink in. Write down each compliment in a journal and how it made you feel. At the end of the week, review these entries and notice how your attitude towards compliments may have shifted.*

Remember, there is a vast difference between arrogance and accepting a compliment. The former involves inflating your accomplishments, while the latter is acknowledging them. By graciously accepting compliments, you're not just showing respect to the person complimenting you; you're showing respect to yourself and acknowledging your own value. And that is a powerful step towards igniting your confidence, positivity, and motivation.

# CHAPTER 61: ENCOURAGING OTHERS: A VIRTUOUS CYCLE

When it comes to igniting your inner spark, personal transformation isn't the only goal; inspiring others is equally important. A little encouragement can have a domino effect, creating a virtuous cycle of positivity, motivation, and self-assurance.

We've all heard the saying, "Rising tides lift all boats." But have you ever stopped to consider the power behind these words? When you take the time to lift up those around you, your actions create a ripple effect. As others grow more confident, positive, and motivated, they, too, are likely to encourage the people in their lives.

This cycle has countless benefits. When you inspire others, you not only contribute to their growth but also strengthen your own sense of purpose, satisfaction, and happiness. The act of giving and receiving encouragement forms a virtuous cycle that enriches everyone's lives.

Now, let's dive into the three main aspects of encouraging others.

## 1. Empowering Others

Empowering others is about recognizing their potential and

supporting their growth. This can involve giving constructive feedback, offering resources, or simply acknowledging their efforts. It's about enabling others to stand on their own and reinforcing their self-belief.

Your journey has undoubtedly taught you many lessons, and sharing these insights can help others navigate their own paths. Remember that your words can serve as a powerful tool. Express faith in people's abilities, encourage them to take risks, and celebrate their achievements, no matter how small.

## 2. Building Connections

Encouragement fosters a sense of community and connection. When we uplift others, we build stronger relationships based on mutual respect and appreciation. This support network not only benefits individual members but also fosters a more positive and empowering environment.

Establish a practice of regularly checking in with those in your network, whether it's a simple "How are you doing?" or a more in-depth conversation about their goals and aspirations. When you take an interest in others, you help them feel valued and understood, laying the groundwork for deeper connections.

## 3. Reaping Mutual Benefits

Lastly, remember that encouraging others also benefits you. It strengthens your empathy skills, enhances your understanding of different perspectives, and reinforces the lessons you've learned. Plus, encouraging others can be incredibly fulfilling.

Now, it's time to put these insights into practice. This week, try to actively encourage at least one person every day. This could be a colleague, a family member, a friend, or even a stranger. Notice how this affects both the recipient and you.

Remember, the spark you kindle in others can create a blaze that lights up the world. Let's set off that virtuous cycle—one word of encouragement at a time.

# CHAPTER 62: MINDFUL EATING: NOURISHING YOUR BODY AND MIND

The journey of confidence, positivity, and motivation isn't just about the mind; it involves the body too. The food we consume directly impacts our physical well-being, our mood, our energy levels, and our mental sharpness. Therefore, it's essential to turn our attention towards mindful eating - an often overlooked but crucial aspect of self-growth.

### Understanding Mindful Eating

Mindful eating is not just about what you eat but how you eat. It involves fully focusing on the experience of eating, savoring every bite, acknowledging your senses, understanding your body's hunger and satiety cues, and expressing gratitude for the nourishment you're receiving.

In our fast-paced world, meals often turn into a mindless act, done while working, watching TV, or on the move. However, when we eat without paying attention, we miss out on the intricate experience of eating and the potential benefits it holds for our health and well-being.

### The Benefits of Mindful Eating

Mindful intentional eating can transform your relationship

with food. It can help you recognize your body's natural hunger signals and differentiate between physical hunger and emotional hunger, preventing overeating and promoting healthier eating habits.

It also encourages slower eating, which is beneficial for digestion and weight management. By fully engaging in the process, mindful eating can enhance the pleasure you derive from food, making each meal a more satisfying experience.

### Practicing Mindful Eating

Starting the practice of mindful eating may seem daunting, but you can start small. Here are some tips to get you started:

Before Eating: Check in with your hunger cues. Are you really hungry, or are you bored, stressed, or eating out of habit?

During Eating: Remove distractions like TV or smartphones. Pay attention to the flavors, textures, and smells. Take smaller bites and chew thoroughly.

After Eating: Take a moment to express gratitude for your meal. Check in with your body again. Are you full? Comfortable? Uncomfortably stuffed?

Remember, the aim is not perfection but awareness. Each meal is a new opportunity to practice mindfulness.

### Nourishment Beyond Food

Mindful eating doesn't stop at nourishing your body; it's also about nourishing your mind. The practice of mindfulness develops your ability to stay present, reduces stress, and promotes a more harmonious relationship with food.

Moreover, mindful eating often leads to healthier food choices as you become more aware of what your body truly needs. As a result, your body gets the right fuel to support your brain function, energy levels, and overall vitality.

### Exercise: Mindful Eating

*Try this exercise at your next meal. First, take a moment to appreciate the look of your food, the colors, and the arrangement. Then, close your eyes as you take your first bite. What flavors can you taste? Is it sweet, sour, salty, or bitter? How's the texture? Is it smooth, crunchy, soft, or firm? Chew slowly, savoring every bit of it. This exercise can heighten your awareness and appreciation for your meals.*

In the quest for confidence, positivity, and motivation, don't forget the food that fuels your journey. By practicing mindful eating, you not only nourish your body but also cultivate a healthier, more balanced relationship with food, enhancing your overall well-being. After all, a healthy body fosters a healthy mind. So, take the time to savor, enjoy, and be present with your food. The benefits may extend far beyond the dining table.

# CHAPTER 63: REDUCING STRESS AND ANXIETY

Have you ever felt a sudden rush of adrenaline during a stressful situation? A quickened heartbeat, sweating palms, and a restless mind are common symptoms of stress and anxiety. The modern world, with its fast pace, high demands, and incessant connectivity, can be a breeding ground for these emotions. However, as we embark on this chapter, remember that stress and anxiety aren't inherently bad. They are our body's response to external pressures, serving as a survival mechanism designed to protect us from threats. The problem arises when these reactions become chronic or disproportionate to the situation at hand. It's this constant, heightened state of stress that can be particularly detrimental to our physical health, mental well-being, and overall quality of life.

### Understanding Stress and Anxiety

To address and reduce stress and anxiety, we first need to understand them. Stress is the body's response to any kind of demand or threat. When you sense danger—whether it's real danger or imagined—the body's hormonal defenses kick into top gear in a rapid, instinctive process known as the "fight-or-flight" stress response.

Anxiety, on the other hand, is a sense of fear, dread, or uneasiness. It can be instigated as a reaction to stress, or it can surface in people who are unable to identify significant stressors in their life. It's an internal warning system to keep us alert and aware, but it can become a problem when it's constantly switched on.

## Acknowledge Your Feelings

Ignoring stress and anxiety won't make them go away. Instead, acknowledge them. Recognize that it's okay to feel these emotions. Acceptance is the first step in addressing and managing them. When you encounter stress or anxiety, ask yourself: What's causing this feeling? Is it an imminent deadline, a challenging relationship, or an upcoming presentation? Identifying the trigger can help you address it head-on.

## Practical Stress and Anxiety Management Techniques

There are numerous strategies and techniques to manage stress and anxiety effectively. Here are a few that you can incorporate into your daily life:

- **Deep Breathing and Mindfulness Meditation:** The practice of mindfulness involves focusing on your current state and living in the 'here and now.' Pairing this with deep breathing exercises can create a relaxation response, a state of profound ease that can be evoked in many ways, including via meditation, yoga, and progressive muscle relaxation.
- **Physical Activity:** Regular exercise is a powerful stress reliever. When you engage in physical activity, your body releases endorphins, the 'feel-good' neurotransmitters, which act as natural painkillers and mood elevators.
- **Balanced Diet:** The decisions you make around the food you eat daily can impact how you feel. Consuming a healthy diet rich in fresh fruits, fresh vegetables, lean proteins, and whole grains can provide you with the

necessary nutrients that help in managing stress.

- **Quality Sleep:** Sleep is your body's time to rest and repair. Lack of adequate sleep can exacerbate feelings of stress and anxiety. Make sure you're getting 7-9 hours of sleep each night.
- **Connect with Others:** Spending time with friends, loved ones, or even pets can release hormones that relieve stress and anxiety. Never underestimate the power of a good chat, a shared laugh, or a warm hug.
- **Practice Self-Care:** Dedicate some time each day to do something that brings you joy and relaxation. This could be reading, gardening, painting, or simply soaking in a warm bath.

Incorporate these strategies into your daily routine. As you do, remember that it's not about completely eliminating stress or anxiety—that's neither possible nor beneficial. It's about learning to manage them in a way that they don't hinder your confidence, positivity, and motivation. You hold the power to control your reactions to life's stressors. Ignite that power, and watch your stress and anxiety diminish as your strength and resilience grow.

### Exercise: Applying Stress Techniques

*Take a moment to identify your most common stressors. Write them down. Next, choose one stress management technique from the list above that you feel you can easily incorporate into your life. Practice it for one week and write down any changes you notice in your stress or anxiety levels.*

Remember, stress and anxiety are parts of life. They are not signs of weakness but signals for us to take a step back, breathe, and care for ourselves. You're on the right path, and with each step, you're developing resilience and a sense of control. You're fueling your inner spark to shine brighter.

# CHAPTER 64: THE POWER OF LIFELONG LEARNING

The Greek philosopher Heraclitus once said, "The only constant in life is change." While this may sound a tad daunting, it brings forward a truth that applies as much to personal growth as it does to the natural world. Change is inevitable, but how we adapt, grow, and evolve with it is entirely up to us. That's where lifelong learning comes in, which is the focus of this chapter.

Lifelong learning is the ongoing, self-motivated pursuit of knowledge, not only for personal or professional development but also for enhancing our understanding of the world around us. It fuels our curiosity, leads to the development of new skills, and opens up fresh perspectives.

### Understanding Lifelong Learning

Lifelong learning is not confined to classrooms or formal education. It's about fostering a mindset of curiosity and openness, always ready to learn something new, from cooking a new dish to understanding a new technology or even learning a new language.

In the context of confidence, positivity, and motivation, lifelong learning plays a significant role. It's a mechanism for personal development, one that cultivates self-confidence through continuous improvement, sparks positivity through the joy of discovery, and fuels motivation by setting and achieving new learning goals.

## Learning as Growth

Think of lifelong learning as a journey towards becoming the best version of yourself. Each new thing you learn adds a layer of knowledge and experience that contributes to your personal growth. It shapes your perspective and opens your mind to new possibilities. The key here is not to learn for the sake of impressing others but for the sheer joy and satisfaction of self-improvement.

## Fostering a Learning Mindset

How can you cultivate a mindset of lifelong learning? Start by acknowledging that you don't know everything - and that's perfectly okay. Understanding that there's always something new to learn is the first step toward adopting this mindset.

Stay curious. Embrace questions. Read widely, delve into new hobbies, and don't shy away from challenges that stretch your comfort zone. These challenges often present the most significant opportunities for learning and growth.

## Practical Ways to Promote Lifelong Learning

Here are a few suggestions to encourage lifelong learning:

- **Read Regularly:** Books, articles, research papers - they're all great sources of knowledge. Explore different genres and topics to broaden your horizons.
- **Take Online Courses:** There are countless online platforms each offering a plethora of courses on a wide array of subjects. Many of these courses are free or relatively inexpensive.
- **Attend Workshops and Seminars**: These can be great opportunities to gain in-depth knowledge about a specific subject and meet like-minded individuals.
- **Learn Through Experience:** Travel, volunteer, or partake in community events. Real-world experiences

provide unique learning opportunities that books or courses often can't offer.

- **Teach Others:** Sharing your knowledge with others not only reinforces what you've learned but also helps build your confidence.

## The Benefits of Lifelong Learning

Adopting a learning mindset and practicing lifelong learning can:

- Increase self-confidence and self-efficacy.
- Enhance resilience, enabling you to adapt to change more easily.
- Increase cognitive flexibility, helping you think out of the box.
- Provide a sense of achievement and fulfillment.
- Foster social connections and improve interpersonal skills.

## Conclusion

Learning is an integral part of our lives. By embracing lifelong learning, you're choosing to stay curious, engaged, and adaptive in a constantly changing world. It's about harnessing the power of knowledge for personal growth and, in the process, boosting your confidence, positivity, and motivation. So, go ahead and ignite your spark of learning and keep it glowing for a lifetime.

# CHAPTER 65: SEEKING MENTORS AND ROLE MODELS

As we ignite the spark of confidence, positivity, and motivation, one important aspect of personal growth that we often overlook is the value of having mentors and role models in our lives. These individuals, often more experienced or skilled, can provide us with insight, guidance, and inspiration, aiding us in our journey toward self-improvement. This chapter will delve into why it's important to seek mentors and role models, how to identify them, and ways to maximize these relationships.

### Why Seek Mentors and Role Models?

Life, as beautiful and complex as it is, doesn't come with an instruction manual. There are countless instances when we feel lost, unsure, or simply in need of advice. This is where mentors and role models come in. They are the lighthouses that guide us through stormy waters, offer valuable insights based on their experiences, and inspire us to be our best selves.

### Identifying Your Mentors and Role Models

Mentors and role models can be anyone who influences your life positively. They can be teachers, leaders, authors, celebrities, friends, family members, or even historical figures. The key is to identify individuals who embody the values you cherish, possess the qualities you admire, or have achieved the goals you aspire to.

When seeking a mentor, consider what you want to learn or achieve. Do you want to advance in your career? Develop a particular skill? Grow spiritually? Your answers will help guide your search for the appropriate mentor.

## Maximizing These Relationships

Building a relationship with a mentor or role model isn't about idolizing them or attempting to replicate their lives. Instead, it's about learning from their experiences, adopting their positive traits, and applying their wisdom to your unique journey.

If you have direct access to your mentor, maintain an open line of communication. Ask questions, seek advice, and most importantly, listen and reflect on their words. If your role models are unreachable or have passed on, you can still learn from them. Read their works, study their actions, and draw inspiration from their lives.

## The Role of Reciprocity

A mentor-mentee relationship is not a one-way street. While mentors provide valuable advice and guidance, mentees can also offer fresh perspectives and renewed passion. This reciprocal relationship allows for mutual growth and learning, making the journey more enriching for both parties.

## The Power of Multiple Mentors

One person does not hold all the answers. It's beneficial to have multiple mentors for different aspects of your life - a career mentor, a fitness mentor, a spiritual mentor, and so forth. This approach enables you to gather diverse insights and learnings.

In conclusion, seeking mentors and role models is a powerful strategy in your personal growth journey. They serve as guiding lights, offering invaluable advice, inspiring us through their actions, and helping us navigate through the intricate pathways of life. As we grow and evolve, we may also find ourselves becoming mentors for others, thus perpetuating the cycle of learning and personal development. As with every aspect of our journey, remember to appreciate the process, honor their contributions, and continually apply the wisdom gained in your quest for self-improvement.

# CHAPTER 66:
# MASTERING YOUR
# MORNING ROUTINE

How you start your day can significantly influence how the rest of it unfolds. It sets the tone, either priming you for success or setting you up for struggle. This is why it's crucial to understand and master your morning routine. As you turn the page on this chapter, you'll explore the role of a healthy morning routine in confidence, positivity, and motivation.

While the idea of a morning routine has been popularized by the viral social media posts of millionaires and high-performing athletes, it is not a one-size-fits-all approach. Your morning routine should be personalized and tailored to your needs, values, and lifestyle. It should be a mindful collection of activities that prepare you for the day ahead, both mentally and physically.

To start, it's crucial to understand the importance of consistency. By creating a routine, you can instill a sense of order and predictability in your life, reducing decision fatigue and stress. Each morning you have a set of tasks to complete; this consistency can foster a sense of accomplishment first thing in the morning, sparking your motivation for the day ahead.

Next, consider including activities that prime your mind for positivity. This could include practices such as meditation, journaling, or affirmations. These methods can help to cultivate a calm, focused mind and encourage a positive outlook on the day ahead.

Physical activities are another essential element to include in your routine. This could be a brisk walk, a yoga session, or a high-intensity workout. The act of moving your body in the morning helps wake up the body, stimulate blood flow, and release mood-enhancing endorphins.

Your routine can also incorporate learning opportunities. Whether that's reading a book, listening to a podcast, or watching a short educational video, investing in your personal development can provide a sense of fulfillment and a confidence boost.

Lastly, consider a nutritional element in your morning routine. This can be a healthy breakfast, a glass of water, or a vitamin supplement. Nourishing your body not only provides the energy for your day but also sends a signal of self-care and self-respect.

To build your personalized routine, start small and gradually add elements over time. Consistency, remember, is key. It's more important to stick to a simple routine every day than to attempt a complex one sporadically. Fine-tune your morning routine, turning the early hours into a foundation for a confident, positive, and motivated day.

Each morning presents a new opportunity, a blank canvas. How you choose to paint it is entirely up to you. Make it a masterpiece.

# CHAPTER 67: EMBRACING CREATIVITY

Creativity is not only a protected domain of artists, musicians, or writers; it is an innate quality within us all. It's an expression of our unique perspective and experience, and tapping into this wellspring can boost our confidence, positivity, and motivation. Welcome to Chapter 67, where we explore the power of embracing creativity.

Creativity allows us to solve problems in novel ways, develop fresh ideas, and express our unique selves. It's a process that requires courage— to face the blank page, the empty canvas, or the silent instrument— but the reward is immense. Each act of creativity is an affirmation of our unique self, which fuels self-confidence and personal growth.

For many, creativity is a pathway to mindfulness and positivity. The act of creating can immerse us in a 'flow' state where we lose ourselves in the process, letting go of past and future concerns. This state can induce calm, positivity, and a sense of achievement that carries over into other aspects of our lives.

But how can you embrace creativity if you don't consider yourself a 'creative' person? The first step is to expand your definition of creativity. If you can solve a problem at work, cook a meal without a recipe, or arrange flowers in a vase, you are being creative. Creativity is not confined to the traditional arts; it's a process of combining existing elements into something new and valuable, and it's a skill you can practice and improve.

To tap into your creativity, set aside regular time for creative activities. This can be anything from doodling, writing a poem, cooking a new recipe, or even creating a new dance routine. It's not about producing a masterpiece; it's about the process and the joy it brings.

Also, foster curiosity and openness in your everyday life. This can include exploring new places, learning about different cultures, and reading widely. These experiences can provide fresh fodder for your creative mind.

Finally, don't fear failure or judgment. Creativity is a personal journey, and what matters most is that it provides you with joy, satisfaction, and a sense of achievement. Embrace the freedom to experiment, make mistakes, and learn from them.

Remember that creativity isn't about competing with others; it's about expressing your unique perspective and reveling in the process. Embracing your creativity can unlock a new level of confidence, positivity, and motivation as you're affirming your individuality and expanding your skills.

Don't forget: you are creative, and the world needs your unique contributions. Embrace creativity, and let it illuminate your path toward self-confidence and personal growth.

# CHAPTER 68: SAVORING LIFE'S LITTLE MOMENTS

Welcome to Chapter 68 of our journey to ignite your confidence, positivity, and motivation. As we have learned so far, embracing various aspects of our lives can empower us, including our creativity, our potential, and our inherent worth. This chapter delves into another key element – the art of savoring life's little moments.

The term "savor" is often used in the context of food and drink to slowly and mindfully enjoy each bite or sip. Similarly, in the context of life, savoring is about deeply appreciating, enjoying, and cherishing our experiences. The capacity to savor the little moments in life not only heightens our enjoyment but also amplifies our gratitude, positivity, and overall well-being.

In our fast-paced world, we often chase after big accomplishments and grand experiences. While these are indeed important, the pursuit of the 'big' can sometimes overshadow the significance of the 'small.' It's the everyday moments, the simple pleasures, that often bring the most joy – the aroma of coffee in the morning, a beautiful sunset, a heartfelt conversation with a friend, or a good book on a rainy day.

Learning to savor these moments cultivates mindfulness, bringing our attention to the present moment without judgment or distraction. When we are fully present, we are more likely to appreciate what we have, fostering an attitude of gratitude. This positive outlook can, in turn, enhance our confidence and motivation as we become more aware of the goodness surrounding us.

How do we cultivate the art of savoring? Here are a few strategies:

- **Mindfulness:** Practice being in the present moment. Try to engage all your senses. What do you see, hear, feel, taste, and smell? When you are fully present, you can appreciate the moment in its entirety.
- **Gratitude:** Make it a habit to acknowledge the good in your life. Perhaps you could keep a gratitude journal, where you note down three things you are grateful for each day.
- **Sharing:** Share your positive experiences with others. This could be through conversation, writing, or social media. Sharing not only amplifies your joy but also spreads positivity.
- **Reflect:** At the end of the day, take a few moments to reflect on the highlights of your day. What brought a smile to your face? What would you like to remember?

Remember, savoring doesn't mean ignoring life's challenges or difficulties. It's about acknowledging that alongside challenges, there are also moments of joy, beauty, and grace, however small they might be. By learning to savor these moments, we nurture a mindset that encourages positivity, boosts our confidence, and fuels our motivation.

As we conclude this chapter, I encourage you to locate a relaxing spot, take a few deep breaths, and reflect on your day. What small moments can you savor? With practice, you'll find that savoring life's little moments can ignite a spark that lights up even the darkest corners, empowering you to live a life full of joy, confidence, and motivation.

# CHAPTER 69: THE IMPORTANCE OF WORK-LIFE BALANCE

We live in a fast-paced world, often priding ourselves on our busyness and productivity. Success, it seems, is measured by how much we achieve professionally and the speed at which we do so. However, this mindset is a slippery slope and can often lead us to a state of burnout, dissatisfaction, and imbalance. In this chapter, we'll explore the importance of work-life balance and how it's not just a lofty ideal but a crucial aspect of your overall well-being.

### The Scale of Balance

Imagine life as a scale, with work on one side and everything else that constitutes life – family, personal time, hobbies, health, friends, and spiritual needs – on the other. When this scale tips too much to one side, we lose balance. In our pursuit of career success, we often fail to recognize this imbalance until the consequences start to manifest themselves – strained relationships, declining health, loss of personal identity, and a decrease in overall happiness.

Understanding and recognizing the symptoms of imbalance is the first step toward achieving a healthier work-life balance. These might include feeling overwhelmed or anxious, perpetual tiredness, neglecting personal responsibilities, or simply finding less joy in activities you once enjoyed.

## Striking the Balance

Achieving a work-life balance doesn't mean dividing your time equally between work and personal life. It's about finding a rhythm that suits your unique circumstances and allows for flexibility. Specific work-life balance will look different for everyone, and that's okay. What's crucial is that you feel fulfilled and happy in both areas of your life.

Here are some practical strategies to start establishing a healthier work-life balance:

- **Set clear boundaries:** In a world where remote work is common and our personal and professional lives often blend, setting boundaries becomes crucial. This could mean having a dedicated workspace at home, setting specific work hours, and avoiding work-related tasks during your off time.

- **Prioritize your time:** Not every task has equal importance. Understand what truly needs your attention and what can wait. Use of tools like to-do lists and calendars can help manage your time effectively.

- **Learn to delegate**: You don't have to do it all, and you can't do it all. Whether it's at work or home, delegate tasks where possible.

- **Take care of your health:** Ensure that you're eating well, exercising, and getting enough sleep. These aspects are often the first to be compromised when work takes precedence, but they are essential for maintaining balance.

- **Make time for relaxation and recreation:** Time spent doing things you love isn't wasted time. It's an investment in your well-being. Schedule specific slots to spend time with your loved ones, set aside time to pursue a hobby, or simply make yourself available to relax.

- **Practice mindfulness:** Be present in what you're doing, whether it's work or leisure. Avoid thinking about work during your off hours and vice versa.

## The Ripple Effect

Work-life balance is not just about your individual well-being. It has a ripple effect on the people around you. A healthy work-life balance enables you to be more present and engaged in your personal relationships and more productive and satisfied in your work.

Understanding that work is a part of life, not all of it, is a perspective shift that can lead to a more balanced and fulfilling life. It's not about compromising your ambitions but about realizing that personal well-being and happiness are essential elements of your overall success.

### Exercises: Values - Identity, Assess, and Plan

*Identify your values: Write down the things that matter most to you in life. This will help guide your decisions and ensure that your actions align with your values.*

*Assess your current work-life balance: Reflect on your current work-life balance. Are there areas where you feel overwhelmed or neglected? How does this make you feel?*

*Plan your week: At the start of each week, plan your time, including work, chores, relaxation, socialization, and personal hobbies. This will help you see how you are currently spending your time and where adjustments need to be made.*

The journey to a balanced life is a personal one and is not always smooth. It's okay to stumble, reassess, and adjust as needed. The goal is not perfection, but a harmonious integration of work and life that fuels, not drains, your spark.

# CHAPTER 70: FOSTERING POSITIVE RELATIONSHIPS

You've been through the journey of igniting your confidence, understanding positivity, and harnessing your motivation, but all this can be significantly amplified by the people you choose to surround yourself with. Hence, chapter 70 shines a spotlight on 'Fostering Positive Relationships.' Relationships make an enormous contribution to our lives; they offer emotional support, shared joy, and growth through mutual experiences and wisdom.

So, how can you foster positive relationships that feed your confidence and positivity rather than drain it?

- **Choose Positivity:** Surround yourself with individuals who uplift you, not those who bring you down. Such people will boost your motivation and confidence, making you feel positive about yourself and your abilities.
- **Mutual Respect**: Ensure that there's mutual respect in your relationships. You cannot build a positive relationship with someone who disrespects you or whom you don't respect. Respecting each other's values, beliefs, and personal space is a cornerstone of positive relationships.
- **Communication is Key:** Communication builds trust and understanding. Be open about your feelings,

thoughts, and ideas, and listen when others share theirs.

- **Support Each Other:** Be there for each other during the tough times as well as the good. Offering support and knowing you can rely on others when you need it helps to foster a positive relationship.
- **Growth Together:** In a positive relationship, both parties should feel they are growing as individuals. Encourage and inspire each other to reach new heights.
- **Healthy Boundaries:** Healthy relationships respect boundaries. Be clear about what you're comfortable with, and ensure you're respecting the boundaries of others.

Reflect on your current relationships, both personal and professional. Are they positive? Do they respect your boundaries, promote growth, and boost your confidence? If not, it might be time for some changes. It could involve a heart-to-heart conversation, setting clearer boundaries, or, in some cases, stepping away from the relationship altogether.

Additionally, strive to build new positive relationships. Meet new people, network in your professional circle, join communities based on your interests and be open to the beautiful relationships you might forge.

As you venture out to foster positive relationships, remember to be a positive influence in others' lives, too. In your interactions, remember the lessons from previous chapters—express empathy, show respect, and offer support. As the saying goes, "Be the change you want to see in the world."

To conclude, nurturing positive relationships can significantly boost your confidence, positivity, and motivation, helping you spark a brighter flame within yourself. Embrace this journey and cherish the positive relationships you'll foster along the way.

# CHAPTER 71: AVOIDING TOXIC PEOPLE AND ENVIRONMENTS

After focusing on the importance of fostering positive relationships, it's equally crucial to understand how to steer clear of the opposite - toxic people and environments. Such influences can diminish your confidence, drain your positivity, and stall your motivation.

Toxicity can be manifested in various ways - constant negativity, disregard for personal boundaries, habitual dishonesty, or persistent emotional manipulation. Recognizing these toxic signs is the first step towards distancing yourself from such damaging influences.

### Recognizing Toxicity

- **Constant Negativity:** Do you have people in your life who always seem to have a negative outlook? Do they tend to downplay your achievements and magnify your mistakes? These can be signs of a toxic person.
- **Disregard for Personal Boundaries**: Toxic individuals may routinely invade your personal space or disregard your boundaries. This can be emotionally draining and harm your self-esteem.
- **Habitual Dishonesty:** Trust is crucial in any

relationship. If you find someone frequently lies or hides the truth, it's a clear sign of toxicity.

- **Persistent Emotional Manipulation:** Emotional manipulation is a common tool used by toxic individuals. They might use guilt, shame, or even flattery to control you or influence your decisions.

### Creating Distance

Once you recognize toxicity, take steps to create distance. It's important to prioritize your emotional health. Here are some strategies:

- **Set Boundaries:** Clearly communicate your boundaries and stick to them. Don't allow anyone to violate these boundaries, regardless of your relationship with them.
- **Limit Interaction:** If possible, limit your interaction with these individuals. Less time spent together means less opportunity for their toxicity to impact you.
- **Seek Support:** Discuss your feelings with a trusted friend, mentor, or counselor. Their guidance and support can be a source of strength.
- **Practice Self-Care:** Ensure you're taking care of your mental, emotional, and physical health. This can help strengthen your resilience against toxic influences.

### Fostering Healthy Environments

Beyond people, toxic environments can also significantly impact your confidence and motivation. These could be physical spaces filled with negativity or digital spaces like social media platforms that foster comparison and criticism.

Recognize these environments and, where possible, distance yourself from them. Seek out positive spaces where you feel uplifted, supported, and motivated.

Remember, it's essential to respect yourself enough to walk away from anything that doesn't serve your growth or happiness. Avoiding toxic people and environments is not about fostering negativity but about protecting your positivity, confidence, and motivation. Keep fueling your spark, and don't let anyone or any environment douse it.

# CHAPTER 72: OVERCOMING PROCRASTINATION

Procrastination is a hurdle we've all encountered. It's a barrier that stands between you and your goals, aspirations, and tasks at hand. It's the comfort of 'later' when the challenge of 'now' feels overwhelming. Overcoming procrastination isn't just about ticking tasks off your to-do list; it's about embracing the strength within you to confront challenges head-on.

### Understanding Procrastination

Procrastination isn't a character flaw or a lack of discipline; it's a response to emotional discomfort. People tend to procrastinate to avoid feelings like boredom, anxiety, insecurity, or frustration that certain tasks might induce.

### Strategies to Overcome Procrastination

- **Break It Down:** Large, complex tasks can be intimidating, pushing you to procrastinate. Break these tasks into manageable parts and start with the easiest part. Each small accomplishment will build your momentum and confidence.
- **The "Two-Minute Rule":** If a task takes two minutes or less to complete, do it immediately. This rule prevents small tasks from piling up and becoming overwhelming.

- **Schedule Your Tasks:** Setting a specific time for a task can make you more likely to follow through. Use reminders to help keep you on track.
- **Eliminate Distractions:** Identify what typically distracts you and take steps to minimize these distractions when you're working on tasks.
- **Self-Compassion:** Don't beat yourself up for procrastinating. Remember, it's a common human tendency. Practicing self-compassion can reduce the guilt you feel about procrastination, which can often lead to more procrastination.
- **Focus on Progress, Not Perfection:** Perfectionism can lead to procrastination by making the fear of making mistakes paralyzing. Emphasize progress and effort instead of a flawless performance.

### Finding Motivation

Overcoming procrastination is closely tied to motivation. Here are a few tips to help build motivation:

- **Visualize Success:** Visualize completing the task successfully. This mental image can provide a motivation boost.
- **Rewards:** Reward yourself when you complete tasks, especially challenging ones. This can make the process more enjoyable and motivating.
- **Positive Affirmations:** Use affirmations to encourage yourself. Telling yourself, "I can do this" or "I am capable and strong" can boost your self-confidence and motivation.

Procrastination can dim your spark, delaying your journey toward increased confidence, positivity, and motivation. By recognizing and combating procrastination, you keep your spark alive and vibrant. Remember, every task completed, no matter how small is a step forward.

# CHAPTER 73: USING TECHNOLOGY TO BOOST CONFIDENCE

As the world has become more connected, technology has become incorporated into nearly every aspect of our lives. From the way we communicate to the way we learn and work, it's ubiquitous. But how can technology be used to boost our confidence, positivity, and motivation?

### Understanding the Role of Technology

Technology, when used effectively, can serve as an incredible tool for self-improvement and growth. It offers a plethora of resources to learn new skills, stay connected, maintain health, and manage our lives more efficiently. It's crucial to harness its power in a way that benefits our journey of personal growth and maintains our well-being.

### Boosting Confidence through Technology

- **Learning New Skills**: Platforms like online courses, tutorials, and webinars can help you acquire new skills or hone existing ones. Achieving these learning milestones can significantly boost your self-confidence.
- **Online Networking:** Engaging in online communities related to your interests or professional field can enhance your self-confidence. Sharing ideas, learning

from others, and receiving positive feedback can validate your capabilities.

- **Health and Fitness Apps:** Keeping track of your physical well-being and reaching health goals can directly influence your self-confidence. Fitness apps, nutrition trackers, or meditation apps can assist in this journey.
- **Digital Vision Boards:** Visualizing your goals can be made easy and interactive with digital vision boards. They serve as a constant, accessible reminder of your ambitions, encouraging progress.
- **Monitoring Progress:** Use digital tools to track your progress toward your goals. Seeing tangible evidence of your efforts can be a powerful confidence booster.

## Avoiding the Pitfalls

While technology can be an enabler, it also has its pitfalls. Social media, for example, if misused, can lead to negative comparisons and decreased self-esteem. It's essential to use these platforms consciously, understanding that people often portray an overly positive, edited version of their lives.

Remember, technology is a tool. Like any tool, its effectiveness depends on how it's used. Using it mindfully and productively can make technology a significant ally in your journey toward increased confidence, positivity, and motivation.

### Exercise: - Positive Tech

*Identify three ways you can use technology to help boost your confidence and make a plan to incorporate these into your routine. Regularly reassess and adjust your usage to ensure it remains a positive influence.*

Technology can be the wind beneath your wings, propelling you toward your goals. Make it your ally, and see your confidence soar.

# CHAPTER 74:
# THE POWER OF
# UNPLUGGING

In a world where our lives are deeply intertwined with technology, it might seem counterintuitive to talk about unplugging. However, as crucial as technology is to our modern existence, setting it aside at times is equally important. This chapter explores the power of unplugging and how it can boost your confidence, positivity, and motivation.

### The Need for Unplugging

Our constant connectivity can often lead to information overload, increased stress, and difficulty focusing on tasks at hand. We may also fall into the trap of unhealthy comparisons and decreased self-esteem due to the carefully curated lives we see on social media. Unplugging, or consciously setting aside technology, helps us regain control and nurture our mental and emotional well-being.

### Boosting Confidence through Unplugging

- **Promoting Mindfulness:** Without digital distractions, we're more present and engaged in our lives. This mindfulness can lead to a more profound appreciation of the world around us, boosting our overall happiness and contentment.
- **Fostering Creativity:** Taking a break from screens can

stimulate our imagination and creativity. When we're not consuming information passively, our minds are free to wander, innovate, and create.

- **Improving Focus:** Unplugging allows us to focus on tasks without distractions, enhancing our productivity and efficiency. Successfully completing tasks can boost our confidence and motivation.
- **Encouraging Real-life Connections:** Face-to-face interactions nurture our need for social connections and can contribute significantly to our emotional health and self-esteem.

### Navigating the Unplugging Process

Unplugging doesn't mean completely giving up technology. It's about setting boundaries and taking regular breaks. Here's how you can navigate the unplugging process:

- **Set Tech-free Times:** Designate specific times of the day when you will not use any digital devices. This might be during meals, the first hour after you wake up, or the hour before you go to bed.
- **Have Tech-free Zones:** Certain areas of your home, like the bedroom or dining area, can be kept free of digital devices.
- **Take Regular Breaks:** For every hour of screen time, take a short break to stretch, move around, or just rest your eyes.
- **Practice Mindful Usage:** Be conscious of your technology usage. Ask yourself if it's necessary, productive, or genuinely entertaining.

### Exercise: Tech-free time

*This week, start with setting aside one hour each day as tech-free time. Notice any changes in your mood, focus, and overall well-being. Gradually, you may increase this duration or add more tech-free intervals.*

Unplugging from technology is like taking a deep breath of fresh air. It gives your mind a chance to rest, rejuvenate, and revive, positively impacting your confidence, positivity, and motivation. Embrace the power of unplugging, and you'll be surprised by the power that lies within you.

# CHAPTER 75: CULTIVATING A POSITIVE ONLINE PRESENCE

In the digital age, our online persona has become a reflection of who we are, extending beyond our physical presence and leaving lasting impressions on others. How you present yourself in the virtual world can significantly influence your confidence, positivity, and motivation. Chapter 75 is dedicated to understanding the importance of cultivating a positive online presence and how it can contribute to your personal growth.

### Understand Your Online Presence

Your online presence comprises everything on the internet that is related to you. This could be a social media profile, blog, or a comment you've made on a public forum. It's crucial to realize that the internet doesn't forget easily; your digital footprint could stay visible for years. Hence, it's essential to ensure you're projecting an image that aligns with your values and promotes positivity.

### Actively Shape Your Digital Image

Creating a positive online presence isn't a passive process. It requires consistent effort to present yourself in a way that reflects your true self, goals, and values. Post content that showcases your interests, achievements, and experiences. Share insights, inspiration, and knowledge that you believe can benefit others. This can help build your confidence as you actively shape your digital identity.

## Digital Positivity

Just as in your daily life, choose positivity online. Encourage others, leave constructive comments, and share uplifting content. Avoid spreading negativity, engaging in conflicts, or participating in destructive criticism. Your online actions can contribute to your personal positivity, affect your mindset, and influence how others perceive you.

## Protect Your Online Reputation

Maintain an awareness of your privacy settings across all platforms. Be discerning about what personal information you share and mindful of how you interact with others. It's essential to deal with any negative aspects of your online presence promptly and professionally. Remember, a healthy online reputation can build credibility and bolster your self-confidence.

## Utilize the Power of Connection

The internet offers untold opportunities to connect with inspiring individuals, groups, and organizations that can motivate you and contribute to your growth. Use this tool to your advantage. Surround yourself with positivity and inspiration, and strive to provide the same for others.

## Reflect and Reset

Regularly review your online presence. Does it accurately reflect who you are and your personal growth? If not, don't hesitate to hit the reset button. Update your profiles, switch up your interactions, or declutter your digital space to maintain a positive, inspiring online presence that reflects the current you.

Throughout this process, remember to extend the kindness, respect, and positivity to others online that you would want reciprocated. In a world increasingly influenced by digital interactions, creating a positive online presence is an investment in your personal growth, self-esteem, and motivation.

### Exercise: Online presence

*Analyze your current online presence. What does it say about you? Is it positive and reflective of who you are? If not, outline three practical steps you could take to improve it.*

# CHAPTER 76: LEARNING TO SAY 'NO'

Life has a funny way of presenting opportunities. While it is natural to grab onto every chance that comes your way, there is an underemphasized power in learning to say 'No.' As we journey through our lives, we encounter countless decisions every day, many of which can shape our lives profoundly. However, the need to please others, fear of rejection, or the dread of missing out often compels us to say 'Yes,' even when we should be saying 'No.'

The power of 'No' isn't about being negative, dismissive, or rude. It is about understanding your priorities, respecting your boundaries, and valuing your time and energy. It is a tool for self-empowerment, reinforcing your self-worth and autonomy.

### The Why of 'No'

Reflect on the last time you agreed to something you didn't want to do. Why did you say 'Yes'? Were you afraid of disappointing someone, or was it an automatic response born out of habit? Understanding the 'why' behind your 'Yes' is the first step towards learning to say 'No.' The insight you gain will help you recognize your patterns and triggers, laying the foundation for change.

### Your Boundaries Matter

You are the curator of your life. You get to decide what goes into it. When you continually say 'Yes' to things that don't align with your values, goals, or interests, you allow your life to be dictated by others. Establishing and respecting personal boundaries isn't selfish; it's an act of self-care. Saying 'No' allows you to safeguard your time, energy, and mental space for the things that truly matter to you.

### Embrace Discomfort

Saying 'No' can feel uncomfortable, especially if you're not used to it. It might bring up feelings of guilt, fear, or anxiety. Embrace this discomfort; it's a sign of growth. With practice, you'll become more comfortable asserting your needs and maintaining your boundaries.

### Communicate Assertively

Communicating your 'No' assertively and respectfully is essential. You don't have to provide lengthy explanations or excuses. A simple "I'm sorry, but I can't commit to this right now" is usually enough. Stand firm in your response, but remain kind and considerate.

### Exercise: Practice Saying 'No'

*Just like any skill, saying 'No' gets easier with practice. Start with smaller, less critical situations, gradually building your confidence to tackle more challenging ones.*

In a world that often demands a 'Yes,' learning to say 'No' is a crucial skill for preserving your energy and maintaining focus on what's truly important. Remember, each 'No' is also a 'Yes' to yourself, your needs, and your priorities. By harnessing the power of 'No,' you make room for the experiences, people, and tasks that truly align with your path to igniting your confidence, positivity, and motivation.

# CHAPTER 77: MAKING PEACE WITH THE PAST

The pages of your life's book are filled with chapters of joy and pain, achievements and setbacks, confidence and self-doubt. Each has played an integral role in shaping who you are today. To continue your journey towards greater self-confidence, positivity, and motivation, it's crucial to make peace with your past. Let's explore how we can accomplish this.

- **Understanding the Past:** You are an amalgamation of your experiences and your reactions to them. The first step to making peace with the past is acknowledging its influence on your present. Your past holds lessons, some of which might be uncomfortable to revisit, yet doing so can bring profound insight. Remember, you aren't your past, but your past is a part of you. Accept this, and you're already on the path to reconciliation.

- **Reshaping Narratives:** When our experiences are emotionally charged, we create narratives around them. It's how we make sense of the world. Some of these narratives might be negative, inhibiting our self-growth and confidence. Look at these narratives with a compassionate, objective eye. Ask yourself if they are serving you well. If not, it's time to reshape them.

- **Forgiving and Letting Go:** Forgiveness, both for ourselves and others, is an essential step in making peace with the past. Holding onto grudges or guilt only anchors you in negativity. By forgiving, you're not condoning wrong actions but rather releasing their hold over you.

- **Creating a Rite of Passage:** Creating a rite of passage is a symbolic act that helps to provide closure. This can take many forms. You might write down your negative experiences and burn the paper as a sign of letting go or plant a tree as a symbol of growth and resilience.
- **Reflection Time:** Take some time to reflect on an experience from your past that may be hindering your self-confidence. What narrative have you created around this event? Is it serving you well, or is it time to reshape it?

### Exercise: Reshape your narrative

*Write down a narrative that you have carried for a long time that doesn't serve you well. Now, reshape that narrative in a positive, empowering way.*

A Past with Peace: Making peace with your past doesn't mean erasing it. It means acknowledging the past, learning from it, and moving forward without allowing it to overshadow your present or future. Remember, the past is a place of reference, not residence.

You are a work in progress, and every step, even the ones backward, are part of your journey. By making peace with your past, you are paving the way for a future filled with greater confidence, positivity, and motivation. Ignite your spark, and keep it glowing brightly. Your past has helped shape you, but it's your actions today that determine who you become tomorrow.

# CHAPTER 78: CULTIVATING OPTIMISM IN DIFFICULT TIMES

Life will inevitably present us with challenges, obstacles, and setbacks. Difficult times test our strength, resilience, and faith. They can make us feel desolate and trapped. Yet, these moments are also ripe for personal growth and transformation. This chapter is about cultivating optimism during such difficult times. It's about transforming our mindset from despair to hope, from fear to courage.

**Understand the Power of Optimism:** Optimism isn't about ignoring the harsh realities of life but rather about choosing to see the potential for growth in every situation. Research has shown that optimism can positively impact both our mental and physical health, improving our ability to cope with stress and even boosting our immunity.

**Acceptance is Key:** Accepting your current situation does not mean resigning to it. Instead, acceptance is about understanding that the hardship is a part of your current reality and releasing resistance against it. This allows you to focus your energy on actions that can improve your circumstances rather than wasting it on denial or resistance.

**Reframe Your Thoughts:** Negative thoughts are a natural response to difficult times. Yet, the way we frame these situations in our minds can significantly impact our experience of them. Try to shift your perspective and see these difficult situations as opportunities for growth, resilience, and self-discovery.

**Cultivate Gratitude:** Even in the darkest times, there's something to be grateful for. Practicing gratitude can shift our focus from what's wrong to what's right, creating space for optimism to thrive. Keep a gratitude journal and make it a habit to note down things you are thankful for daily.

**Surround Yourself with Positivity:** The company we keep can greatly influence our mindset and attitude. Surround yourself with positive, optimistic people who can support and uplift you during difficult times. Their positive energy can help reinforce your own optimism.

**Set Realistic Expectations:** Sometimes, our own unrealistic expectations can lead to disappointment and negative thinking. It's important to set achievable goals and manage expectations to nurture optimism.

**Maintain a Healthy Lifestyle: Optimism** isn't just about mental well-being; it's closely tied to physical health as well. Regular focused exercise, an intentional healthy diet, and enough sleep can boost your mood, energy, and overall outlook on life, making it easier to cultivate optimism.

**Practice Mindfulness:** Being present and engaged in the current moment prevents you from dwelling on past mistakes or worrying about the future. Mindfulness techniques, such as focused meditation or deep breathing, can aid in grounding you in the present moment and foster a more optimistic mindset.

To conclude, cultivating optimism in difficult times is not about unreasoning positivity but rather a conscious decision to keep hope alive. It's about embracing life's challenges as opportunities for growth and believing in your ability to overcome. Remember, darkness is always deepest before dawn. Cultivate optimism, keep faith, and soon you will find the strength to step into the light.

## Exercise: Reframing challenges

*Think about a challenging situation in your life. How might you reframe it as an opportunity for growth? Write down three positive aspects or potential outcomes of this situation to help foster your sense of optimism.*

Affirmation: "I choose to see the potential for growth in every situation. I am resilient, and I will overcome my challenges with optimism and grace."

# CHAPTER 79:
# FINDING PURPOSE
# IN YOUR WORK

"Choose a job you love, and you will never have to work a day in your life." – Confucius.

The significance of this quote doesn't lie in the avoidance of work but in the pursuit of purpose and passion. Finding purpose in your work can be a catalyst for confidence, positivity, and motivation. In this chapter, we will delve into understanding the essence of purposeful work and how you can discover your own work-related purpose.

Purpose is a powerful motivator. When you see your work as a vehicle for making a difference, it no longer feels like a chore. Instead, it becomes a meaningful journey, a personal mission. Studies show that individuals who consider their work meaningful are more likely to be engaged, productive, and satisfied.

## Identifying Your Purpose

To find purpose in your work, you need first to understand what drives you. This is typically a combination of your values, passions, and strengths. Reflect upon the moments when you feel most fulfilled - when time seems to fly and you are engrossed in your work. What kind of tasks are you performing? Who are you helping? What problems are you solving? By dissecting these instances, you can identify the key elements that give your work purpose.

## Aligning Your Work with Your Purpose

Once you've identified what gives you a sense of purpose, the next step is to align this with your work. This may involve seeking new opportunities within your current job, or it might mean considering a career change. Regardless, the goal is to ensure that your work isn't just a way to pay the bill but a platform to express your values and make a meaningful impact.

## Making a Difference

Remember that even the smallest tasks can contribute to a larger purpose. For example, if you value helping others, you might find purpose in a role that involves customer service. If you are passionate about innovation and problem-solving, you might find purpose in roles that allow you to design and create.

## Persevering through Challenges

Finding and following your purpose isn't always a smooth path. There will be challenges and moments when you question whether the struggle is worth it. In these moments, it's important to remind yourself of your 'why' - the core reason that you're doing what you're doing. This 'why' can serve as a guiding star, helping you navigate through the most challenging times.

### Exercise: Identifying Your Work-Related Purpose

*Take a moment to think about your current work situation. Write down the aspects of your job that align with your personal values and passions. If you're struggling to find any, don't despair. Consider the skills you've developed, the people you've met, or the lessons you've learned. No experience is ever wasted.*

*Next, write down your dream job - the role you would love to be in if there were no limitations. What does it involve? How does it align with your passions and strengths? How does it contribute to the world in a way that matters to you?*

*Now, compare these two descriptions. Is there a gap? If so, what steps could you take to bridge this gap? What skills might you need to develop? What connections might you need to make? Don't worry about creating a detailed plan; simply start considering the possibilities.*

Remember, finding purpose in your work is a journey, not a destination. It may take time and effort, but the rewards - in terms of satisfaction, motivation, and happiness - are truly invaluable. As you move forward in your career, continually revisit and refine your sense of purpose. This ongoing process of reflection and realignment will help keep your spark ignited, fueling your journey to a fulfilling work life.

# CHAPTER 80:
# BUILDING TRUST
# AND CREDIBILITY

As you journey through this life, one factor that significantly influences your confidence, positivity, and motivation is trust —both in yourself and others—and the credibility you hold. Trust is not an abstract concept but rather an emotional state that dictates the nature of your relationships and the way others perceive you. Credibility, on the other hand, is the amount of trust others place in you based on your track record, your integrity, and your abilities. Together, these elements create an environment that fosters mutual respect, encourages collaboration, and enhances your overall personal growth.

## Understanding Trust and Credibility

Trust begins with self. Do you trust in your abilities, decisions, and instincts? Do you trust in your capacity to navigate through difficult situations and make the right choices? This internal trust forms the foundation of external trust, which is how much others believe in you. Your credibility, on the other hand, is your reputation—it's how others perceive you based on your past actions and demonstrated competencies.

## How Trust Influences Your Life

Trust influences nearly every aspect of your life. When you trust yourself, you're able to face challenges with confidence.

Self-trust also empowers you to set and maintain healthy boundaries, fostering positive relationships with others.

Externally, trust helps build strong relationships, whether professional or personal. It encourages open communication, cooperation, and mutual understanding, all of which are critical for personal and professional success.

## Building Trust and Credibility

Building trust and credibility takes time and conscious effort. Here are a few ways you can work on them:

- **Consistency:** Consistency in your actions, behavior, and words helps others to predict your responses, which in turn builds trust.
- **Honesty:** Honesty promotes transparency and understanding. Even when the truth is difficult to communicate, honesty fosters respect and trust.
- **Reliability:** Doing what you say you'll do demonstrates reliability. If you promise to deliver, ensure you fulfill that promise.
- **Competence:** Develop your skills and continue to learn and grow in your chosen fields. Demonstrating your competence consistently boosts your credibility.
- **Integrity:** Uphold your values and principles even when no one's watching. Integrity builds a solid reputation that earns the trust of others.

## Trust, Credibility, and Confidence

As you build trust and credibility, you'll notice a significant improvement in your self-confidence. When you trust yourself, your abilities, and your decisions, it's easier to remain confident even in challenging situations. Additionally, as you earn credibility and receive positive feedback from others, it will reinforce your self-belief and boost your confidence further.

## Exercise: Rebuild Trust

*Reflect on your current level of self-trust. Are there areas where you doubt yourself unnecessarily? Write down these areas and brainstorm ways you can start to rebuild trust in those aspects of your life. Remember, self-trust forms the foundation for external trust and credibility.*

## Keep Growing

Building trust and credibility is a continuous process that requires consistency, honesty, reliability, and integrity. This journey may take time, but the rewards it brings to your life —enhanced relationships, improved self-confidence, increased positivity, and motivation—are worth every effort.

Trust in yourself, cultivate credibility, and watch as the world opens up to you. You have the power to shape your life's narrative, so let it be one of trust, credibility, and unwavering confidence. Keep your spark ignited, and continue to shine.

# CHAPTER 81: EMBRACING PERSONAL GROWTH

Personal growth is the life-long journey of understanding and developing oneself to achieve one's fullest potential. It is a vital part of human life and is intertwined with the feelings of self-fulfillment and happiness. Just as a tree continues to grow, pushing its roots deep into the ground while reaching for the sky, humans also have an inherent need for growth. This chapter is designed to help you understand the importance of embracing personal growth, including the role it plays in shaping everyones life, and how to make it a consistent part of your journey.

Personal growth does not happen in a vacuum. It is fostered through new experiences, challenges, and the acquisition of knowledge and skills. It is the process of becoming better, stronger, more knowledgeable, and more self-aware. Personal growth often involves stepping outside of your comfort zone, trying new things, and welcoming change, even when it feels uncomfortable.

Embracing personal growth means acknowledging that there is always room for improvement. It's about seeing life as a continuous learning journey and striving to learn and grow in every situation. Whether we are dealing with triumphs or trials, each experience offers unique lessons that can help us grow.

However, personal growth is not just about becoming 'better' or reaching for an ideal self. It also involves understanding and accepting your limitations and weaknesses. Knowing where you fall short allows you to make conscious efforts to improve or manage these areas. It's about balance between striving for more and accepting where you are.

Here are some strategies that can help you embrace personal growth:

- **Set Personal Goals:** Goals give you a sense of direction. They provide focus and allow you to measure progress. Whether you want to improve a skill, learn something new, or make a lifestyle change, setting specific, clear and achievable goals is the first step.
- **Adopt a Growth Mindset:** This means viewing challenges as opportunities rather than obstacles and believing that your abilities can be developed through dedication and hard work.
- **Practice Self-Reflection:** Take time to reflect on your experiences, thoughts, and feelings. Reflection helps in understanding oneself better and promotes self-awareness, which is essential for personal growth.
- **Embrace Change:** Change can be scary but also a sign of growth. Welcoming change allows you to adapt and learn from different situations.
- **Learn Continuously:** Never stop learning. Whether it's through books, courses, or experiences, continual learning expands your knowledge and perspective.
- **Seek Feedback:** Constructive criticism can be a powerful tool for growth. It can provide insights into areas you may need to work on.

Remember, personal growth is an ongoing continuous journey, not a destination. It's about progress, not perfection. Embrace every part of this journey, even the challenging parts. Each step you take towards personal growth is a step towards a more fulfilling and enriched life.

In the following pages, you'll find guided exercises and prompts to help you understand your personal growth journey better and formulate a strategy to make personal growth a consistent part of your life.

# CHAPTER 82: DEVELOPING LEADERSHIP SKILLS

Just as the brightest spark can light up the darkest night, an individual who ignites their confidence, positivity, and motivation can influence and lead others towards the same path. This is the foundation of effective leadership, a quality that can transform not just your life but also the lives of others. Leadership isn't solely about having a high-rank position or title; it's about inspiring, empowering, and guiding others.

Leadership skills are not reserved for the chosen few. We all have the potential to become leaders in various aspects of our lives - be it at home, work, or within our communities. This chapter will help you develop these leadership skills by focusing on empathy, communication, motivation, and resilience.

## Empathy: A True Leader's Asset

Effective leadership is deeply rooted in empathy, the ability to put yourself in the shoes of others and understand and share their feelings. Empathy allows you to connect with others on an emotional level, making you more approachable and trustworthy. It involves listening intently, validating others' experiences, and responding with kindness and understanding.

### Exercise: Active Listening
*To cultivate empathy, spend a week actively practicing active listening. In conversations, focus on understanding the other*

*person's perspective instead of preparing your response. Ask questions that show your interest and help you understand better.*

## Communication: The Bridge to Understanding

Good communication is essential in leadership. It's how you clearly and effectively convey your thoughts, ideas, and expectations. It's not just about speaking; it's also about listening and understanding others.

### Exercise: Assertiveness & Listening
*Activity: Improve your communication skills by practicing assertive communication. Start by expressing your thoughts in a clear, straightforward, and respectful manner. Then, work on your listening skills, focusing on understanding rather than just responding.*

## Motivation: Igniting the Spark in Others

As a leader, one of your key roles is to inspire and motivate others. By creating a positive and encouraging environment, you can help others ignite their own sparks.

### Exercise: Inspirational qualities
*Think of someone who inspires you and identify what it is about them that motivates you. Can you adopt these qualities? Furthermore, provide positive feedback and encouragement to those around you.*

## Resilience: Leading Through the Storms

Leadership involves navigating through challenges and uncertainties. Developing resilience—the ability to bounce back from adversity—is a key leadership skill. Resilient leaders remain calm under pressure, adapt to change, and view failures as opportunities to learn and grow.

Cultivate resilience by adopting a growth mindset. When you encounter challenges, view them as opportunities for growth rather than obstacles.

Remember, developing leadership skills is a journey, not a destination. Like igniting a spark, it requires patience, effort, and the right tools. As you work on these skills, you'll not only become a better leader, but you'll also boost your confidence, positivity, and motivation, inspiring others to do the same. So, go ahead and lead the way to a brighter, more enlightened path.

# CHAPTER 83: UNDERSTANDING THE IMPORTANCE OF PLAY

In a world that often values productivity over all else, we have been conditioned to perceive play as a frivolous luxury rather than a vital component of a balanced life. We are taught to believe that play is for children while work is for adults. But is it really so? Welcome to Chapter 83, where we rekindle our understanding of the importance of play and how it fosters our overall confidence, positivity, and motivation.

### The Power of Play

Play, in essence, is a state of mind where you engage in an activity for pure enjoyment, fun and recreation rather than for a serious or practical purpose. It is about immersing oneself in the joy of the present moment. While it may seem counterintuitive, this 'non-serious' act has serious benefits. It serves as a powerful catalyst for creativity, stress reduction, and improved brain function.

### Unleashing Creativity

Play is the mother of innovation. When we allow ourselves to experiment, make mistakes, and explore possibilities without the constraints of 'right' and 'wrong,' we foster our innate ability to think outside the box. Whether it's playful brainstorming in a team meeting, doodling in your notebook, or taking a playful approach to problem-solving, embracing play can stimulate our creative faculties in unprecedented ways.

## Alleviating Stress

When was the last time you were truly engrossed in a fun-filled activity? Do you remember how it made you feel? The lightness of being, the reduced tension, and the infectious laughter are nature's best stress busters. It's a fantastic way to disconnect from everyday worries and allow your mind and body to rejuvenate.

## Enhancing Brain Function

Play isn't just for kids. Engaging in playful activities stimulates our brains, helping to improve memory, focus, and cognitive function. It is also believed that play can slow down the aging process and increase overall life satisfaction.

## Finding Your Play

Play is personal and unique to every individual. It could be dancing, painting, playing a musical instrument, gardening, hiking, or even a playful mindset at work. The possibilities are endless.

### Exercise: Playtime

*Now, this is your invitation to play. Take out a moment to reflect on your favorite playful activities from your childhood. Can you pick up one or more of these activities again? Or maybe you would like to explore something entirely new. Set aside some time in your daily or weekly routine to engage in these playful pursuits.*

*Remember, it's not about mastering a skill or achieving a goal but about immersing yourself in the joy of the activity. Approach it with an open heart, a curious mind, and a playful spirit.*

In the hustle of life, let's not forget to play. Remember the words of George Bernard Shaw: "We don't stop playing because we grow old; we grow old because we stop playing." So, go ahead and unleash your inner child. Let your life be touched by the magic of play.

The next chapter will help you understand how to overcome social anxiety, which may be a barrier to fully expressing and embracing your playful side in various social settings. Until then, keep playing, keep exploring, and keep igniting your Spark.

# CHAPTER 84: OVERCOMING SOCIAL ANXIETY

As we continue our journey through this compendium of self-discovery and growth, we now arrive at Chapter 84: Overcoming Social Anxiety.

Social anxiety is a common but deeply personal challenge that many of us face. It's the fear or apprehension that can seize us when we think about or are in social situations. It often manifests in an assortment of different ways, from a minor nervous flutter in our stomachs before a public presentation to an overwhelming dread of any social interaction.

So, how do you combat this fearsome foe? How can you transform social anxiety into social confidence? Let's explore this together.

### Recognize and Understand Your Fear

The first step in overcoming any fear, including social anxiety, is to recognize and understand it. Fear has a funny way of shrinking when we look it directly in the eyes. Write down the situations that make you anxious and try to identify what exactly about them causes you distress. Is it fear of judgment, fear of making a mistake, or fear of the unknown? Understanding and acknowledging your fear is the first step towards conquering it.

### Reframe Your Mindset

One of the most powerful techniques for overcoming social anxiety is cognitive restructuring, a fancy term for changing the way you think about things. Rather than seeing social situations as threatening, try to reframe them as opportunities for learning, growth, and connection. This might sound difficult, but with practice, it can become second nature.

### Start Small and Practice

Like any other skill, socializing improves with practice. Start with smaller, less intimidating situations. Maybe that means striking up a conversation with a cashier, attending a small gathering of close friends, or simply making eye contact and smiling at a stranger. Gradually exposing yourself to social situations can help desensitize your anxiety response over time.

### Use Relaxation Techniques

Techniques to aid relaxation include deep breathing, progressive muscle relaxation, and mindfulness. All of these can all help reduce feelings of anxiety. Experiment with different techniques to see what works best for you, and use them when you start to feel your anxiety creeping up.

### Self-Compassion and Self-Care

Remember to be kind to yourself throughout this process. Overcoming social anxiety isn't easy, and it's okay to have bad days. Practice self-care and self-compassion. Reward yourself for small victories, and don't beat yourself up if progress seems slow.

### Seek Support

Sometimes, we all need a little help. If your social anxiety feels overwhelming, seeking professional help from a good therapist or counselor can be incredibly beneficial. They can provide you with effective strategies and new tools to identify and manage your anxiety, and to improve your social skills.

To conclude this chapter, it's worth remembering that the goal isn't to completely eradicate social anxiety (a little bit of nerves can be a good thing!) but rather to prevent it from controlling your life.

## Exercise: Facing a social situation

*Your challenge for this chapter is to put one of these techniques into practice. Choose a social situation that you usually avoid due to anxiety and face it head-on using the tools you've learned. It might be nerve-wracking, but remember, you're taking a bold step toward igniting your spark of confidence.*

Stay tuned for the next chapter, where we'll delve into the concept of cultivating an abundance mindset. This journey is filled with exciting turns and opportunities for growth, and we're thrilled to be on it with you!

# CHAPTER 85: CULTIVATING AN ABUNDANCE MINDSET

We've all heard the phrase "mind over matter," and nowhere is this more relevant than when it comes to shaping our mindset. Our perceptions and attitudes towards life can dramatically impact our experiences and outcomes. This chapter focuses on one of the most transformative perspectives to adopt: the Abundance Mindset.

The Abundance Mindset, a term that has been popularized by Stephen Covey in his best-selling book, "The 7 Habits of Highly Effective People," refers to the belief that there are plenty of resources, successes, and opportunities for everyone. It contrasts with the Scarcity Mindset, which views life as a zero-sum game where if one person gains, another loses.

People with an Abundance Mindset approach life with positivity, generously share their resources, and believe in their ability to create opportunities. They feel grateful for what they have and are confident about future prospects, which in turn attracts more positivity and opportunity into their lives.

Transitioning from a mindset of scarcity to an abundance mindset is not always straightforward. It requires persistent effort and a willingness to question deep-seated beliefs. But the rewards – increased positivity, better relationships, improved resilience, and higher motivation – make the journey worth it.

## Acknowledge Your Existing Mindset

Begin by understanding your existing mindset. Do you often feel like opportunities are limited, or do you believe there's always another chance around the corner? Do you find yourself often comparing your life with others, or do you celebrate others' success? Recognizing your current mindset is the first step toward change.

## Practice Gratitude

Gratitude shifts your focus from what's missing in your life to appreciating what you have. It's one of the most effective ways to foster an abundance mindset. Consider starting a gratitude journal where you record three things you're grateful for every day.

## Expand Your Perspective

Broaden your worldview by exposing yourself to diverse ideas, cultures, and philosophies. Reading, traveling, and meeting new people can help you understand that the world is full of opportunities and varied ways of living and thinking.

## Affirm Abundance

Affirmations are a powerful tool in reshaping our beliefs. Use affirmations like "I attract success," "There is plenty for everyone, including me," or "I am open to new opportunities." Over time, these statements can shape your subconscious thinking and cultivate an abundance mindset.

## Generosity: Give to Get

Generosity is a powerful demonstration of an abundance mindset. When you give, you are acting out of abundance, not scarcity. And often, you'll find that the more you give, the more you receive in return. This isn't about expecting something in return for your giving but recognizing that generosity creates a positive feedback loop that enriches your life and the lives of others.

Remember, an abundance mindset doesn't mean denying life's challenges or adopting an overly optimistic view. Instead, it's about acknowledging the full spectrum of life's experiences while choosing to focus on possibilities and abundance. Cultivating an abundance mindset won't happen overnight. Be patient with yourself. It's a process, and even small shifts can have a significant impact. As you move forward, you'll start to notice how this mindset affects your outlook, your decisions, and your ability to seize opportunities you might have otherwise overlooked.

# CHAPTER 86: TAKING RESPONSIBILITY FOR YOUR ACTIONS

As we continue our journey towards a more confident, positive, and motivated self, it's essential to develop a healthy relationship with responsibility. Owning our actions, both good and bad, is a vital aspect of growth and self-improvement.

Taking responsibility isn't about dwelling on your failures or beating yourself up over mistakes. Instead, it's about understanding that you are the architect of your life, and your actions have a direct impact on the outcomes you experience.

### The Power of Accountability

When you take responsibility for your actions, you become accountable for the consequences that follow, whether they're positive or negative. This sense of accountability allows you to feel in control of your life as you recognize the power you hold over your future.

Responsibility also breeds integrity. By acknowledging your actions and their impact on others, you demonstrate honesty and authenticity, key traits that build trust and respect in personal and professional relationships.

### Learning from Mistakes

Everyone makes mistakes. But what separates the individuals who grow from those who stagnate is their approach to these errors. Taking responsibility for your actions means acknowledging your missteps, learning from them, and making a conscious effort to avoid repeating them in the future. This process facilitates personal growth and helps you navigate life more effectively.

## Taking Positive Actions

On the flip side, taking responsibility also means celebrating your successes and understanding the actions that led to positive outcomes. By recognizing the behaviors that contribute to your success, you can continue to implement these actions and cultivate a pattern of positivity and progress.

## The Responsibility-Confidence Connection

Taking responsibility for your actions enhances your confidence. As you learn to trust yourself in decision-making and action-taking, you'll feel a greater sense of control and assurance in your abilities.

## Practical Steps to Take Responsibility

Begin by acknowledging both your achievements and mistakes. Celebrate your wins, and examine your failures without judgment. Use them as opportunities for learning and improvement.

When you find yourself in a challenging situation, instead of looking outward to place blame, look inward. Ask yourself, "What could I have done differently?" This mindset shifts you from a victim mentality to an empowered one.

Regularly practice self-reflection. Take time to review your day or week, evaluating your actions and their outcomes. Use this information to guide your future behavior.

Lastly, when you do make a mistake, apologize sincerely and make amends when possible. Remember, everyone, errs, but not everyone has the courage to admit it and take corrective action.

In conclusion, taking responsibility for your actions is a crucial step in cultivating confidence, positivity, and motivation. By owning your actions and their consequences, you assert control over your life and build a strong foundation for personal growth and success. This chapter might have been a challenging read, but it's a crucial lesson on the path toward igniting your inner spark.

# CHAPTER 87: TRANSFORMING ENVY INTO MOTIVATION

Life is a plethora of emotions, some being easier to embrace than others. Envy, one of the more challenging emotions, often leaves us feeling inferior or discontent. This chapter will teach you how to transmute envy into a powerful force of motivation, assisting your growth and advancement in various aspects of life.

We first need to understand that feeling envious is an inherent part of human nature. We all have experienced that pang of longing when we see someone achieving what we've been striving for. However, the secret to transforming this emotion lies in accepting it as a natural response and not an indication of personal failure or inadequacy.

Consider envy as a compass, pointing towards areas in your life that you feel need enhancement or focus. It might be indicating unfulfilled ambitions or desires that you may not have even acknowledged yet. Use this information to create a roadmap for self-improvement, channeling your energy positively.

To do this, start by identifying what specifically triggers your envy. Is it someone's successful career, their fitness level, their relationships, or perhaps their apparent self-confidence? These aspects are clues to what you subconsciously desire.

Once you've pinpointed these areas, use them as fuel for your motivation. For instance, if you envy someone's career success, it might be a sign that you crave growth in your professional life. To achieve this, you could seek out further education, mentorship, or additional responsibilities at work.

Transforming envy into motivation also involves shifting your mindset. Instead of viewing others' success as a testament to your failure, see it as proof that your goal is achievable. Remember, their journey is not a mirror image of yours but an example of what's possible.

It's important to note that everyone has their struggles, and what you see on the surface may not reflect the complete picture. This perspective helps demystify the illusion that everyone else is experiencing unparalleled success while you're left behind. We're all on unique paths, each with its own pace and obstacles.

While channeling envy into motivation, ensure you also celebrate your own progress, however small it may seem. Rejoicing in your victories, practicing gratitude, and focusing on your unique strengths can decrease feelings of envy and amplify feelings of self-confidence.

### Exercise: Transform envy into motivation.

*Find a quiet space and jot down three things you often find yourself envious of. For each item, write down one actionable step you can take towards achieving it. Commit to taking these steps in the next week.*

By understanding the roots of our envy and using it as a motivation tool, we can shift from a state of longing to one of empowerment. As you navigate your journey of self-improvement, remember that the feeling of envy is not a mark of failure but a signpost pointing you toward your desired destination.

# CHAPTER 88:
# HANDLING CRITICISM

Criticism is an unavoidable part of life. It comes from all directions - from our bosses, colleagues, family, friends, and even strangers. It can be constructive or destructive, solicited or unsolicited. The way we respond to criticism and how we handle it is what truly defines us. Instead of perceiving it as a threat, it's crucial to see it as an opportunity for growth and self-improvement. In this chapter, we'll explore the art of handling criticism with grace, acceptance, and optimism.

### Understanding Criticism

Criticism can be hard to digest, primarily because it involves a judgment or assessment that questions our abilities or actions. It can trigger self-doubt and insecurity, and these feelings often elicit a defensive response. However, it's essential to understand that not all criticism is negative. Constructive criticism aims to help us improve and evolve, to better ourselves and our performance. On the other hand, destructive criticism, often based on personal judgments or biases, serves no such purpose. The first step to handle criticism effectively is to distinguish between these two types.

### Accepting and Learning from Constructive Criticism

Constructive criticism is a precious gift. It can provide a fresh perspective, shed light on hidden spots, and offer a path to development. Here are a few tips to handle constructive criticism:

**Listen**: Fully listen to the critique without interruption or defensive counterarguments. Understand the essence of what's being said, and ask for clarification if necessary.

**Reflect**: Give yourself time to process the feedback. Evaluate its merits and applicability objectively.

**Respond**: Instead of reacting impulsively, respond thoughtfully. Thank the person for their feedback, even if you don't agree with everything said.

**Act**: If you find the criticism valid, act on it. Implement the suggestions, seek additional resources if needed, and track your progress.

### Handling Destructive Criticism

Destructive criticism can be hurtful and demoralizing. However, it's vital to remember that this kind of criticism often says more about the critic than the person being criticized. Here's how to handle it:

- **Stay Calm:** Keep your emotions in check. Resist the urge to react impulsively or defensively.

- **Evaluate:** Assess the criticism. Is there any truth in it, or is it just someone's unfounded opinion?

- **Discard or Learn:** If the criticism seems biased or unfair, dismiss it. But, if there's a kernel of truth, even in destructive criticism, consider that as an area to improve.

- **Practice Empathy:** Often, destructive criticism stems from a person's insecurities, frustrations, or personal issues. Empathize without accepting the negativity.

In all of this, remember that your personal value is not reduced based on someone else's inability to appreciate your worth.

Criticism is an external feedback; it should not dictate your self-worth or self-esteem. Instead, use it as a tool for self-improvement and personal growth.

## Exercise: Handling Criticism

*To practice handling criticism, try this simple exercise. The next time you receive criticism, jot down your immediate feelings and thoughts. Wait for a while until your emotions have settled, then revisit what was said. Evaluate it objectively, and plan your response and course of action. This will help you develop a healthier and more constructive relationship with criticism.*

In the next chapter, we will navigate life's inevitable transitions and the role they play in our ongoing journey of self-discovery and growth.

# CHAPTER 89:
# COPING WITH LIFE
# TRANSITIONS

Life is a journey of constant change. From seemingly insignificant daily changes to significant life transitions such as graduating, changing jobs, starting a new relationship, becoming a parent, or moving to a new city, change is a constant companion. Some changes are planned, while others occur unexpectedly, pushing us into a whirlwind of emotions and uncertainties. Learning to cope with these life transitions is a crucial part of maintaining and igniting your confidence, positivity, and motivation.

Life transitions can stir up a range of emotions, from exhilaration and anticipation to anxiety, sadness, or fear. While these emotions are normal, it's essential to navigate them in a healthy way. Ignoring or suppressing your feelings can lead to stress, anxiety, or even physical health problems. Instead, acknowledge your emotions, allow yourself to feel them, and then consider what these emotions are telling you. Remember, it's okay to feel uncertain or scared, and it's equally okay to feel excited or hopeful.

Now, let's explore some strategies to navigate life transitions successfully:

- **Maintain a Positive Outlook:** It's easy to become overwhelmed by the uncertainties that come with change. However, adopting a positive outlook can help you see the potential opportunities that every transition brings. Instead of focusing on what you're leaving behind, try to concentrate on what you're moving toward. Every change is an opportunity for growth and new experiences.

- **Take Care of Your Physical Health**: Significant transitions have been known to take a toll on physical well-being if you're not careful. Ensure you're getting adequate rest, eating nutritious food, and staying active. Taking care of your body can provide the energy and resilience needed to handle transitions effectively.

- **Rely on Your Support Network**: Reach out to your friends, family, or a mentor during a transition period. Having someone to talk to can provide comfort, practical advice, and a fresh perspective.

- **Maintain Familiar Routines**: Amid the flux of a significant transition, maintaining some familiar routines can provide a sense of stability and normalcy. Whether it's your morning exercise, nightly reading, or a weekly call with a loved one, these routines can be grounding anchors.

- **Practice Mindfulness**: Embrace the present moment and avoid excessive worry about the future. Mindfulness can help manage stress, increase emotional awareness, and improve overall well-being during a transition.

- **Acceptance**: Accept that change is part of life and that it's okay to feel unsettled during a transition. Acknowledging this can help lessen resistance to change and foster the resilience necessary to adapt successfully.

Life transitions can be challenging, but they are also opportunities for growth and self-discovery. As you navigate these changes, remember the core principle of our journey through this book: belief in yourself. Trust your ability to adapt, grow, and thrive. It's through navigating these transitions that we often find our strength, learn to appreciate the constants in our lives, and recognize the transformative power of change. As the saying goes, "The only way to make sense out of change is to plunge into it, move with it, and join the dance."

# CHAPTER 90: CULTIVATING INNER PEACE

Welcome to Chapter 90 of your journey. It's been quite a ride, hasn't it? As we travel through life, we come to understand that not all is in our control. The world can feel chaotic, and we can sometimes feel swept along by the current of events. This chapter invites you to discover a place of tranquility amidst the chaos - your inner peace.

### The Haven Within

You might wonder, what is inner peace? Is it achievable? How does it relate to my confidence, positivity, and motivation? Inner peace, simply put, is a state of mental and emotional tranquility. It's an inner sanctuary where worry, stress, and anxiety do not rule. It's the ability to remain calm and composed, even amidst chaos. Inner peace amplifies your confidence, allows positivity to flourish, and fuels your motivation.

### Chasing Peace, Finding Chaos

Why is inner peace so elusive? We live in a fast-paced world where the chase for success, wealth, and recognition is often unending. The constant pressure to 'do more' and 'be more' can lead to restlessness and anxiety.

Peace isn't found by chasing after external circumstances or desires. It's discovered within by aligning with your authentic self and honoring your own journey. Inner peace doesn't mean you stop striving for goals or overcoming challenges. It means doing so in a way that doesn't disturb your tranquility.

## Cultivating Inner Peace

- **Awareness:** The first step towards inner peace is awareness. Recognize the moments when you are feeling anxious or stressed. Acknowledge them without judgment and gently remind yourself that your inner peace is important.
- **Mindfulness and Meditation:** We've talked about mindfulness and meditation before, but they're worth mentioning again. These practices guide us to focus on the present moment and detach from negative thoughts, nurturing a peaceful state of mind.
- **Acceptance:** Acceptance does not mean passivity or resignation. It means understanding that there are things beyond our control. You can only control your actions and reactions. Focus on these and let go of the rest.
- **Gratitude:** Embracing a spirit of gratitude can significantly enhance inner peace. It shifts our focus from what we lack to the abundance we already have.
- **Forgiveness**: Holding onto resentment and anger disturbs inner peace. Practicing forgiveness, both towards yourself and others, cultivates tranquility.
- **Balance**: Strive for a healthy balance in all areas of your life - work, relationships, personal time, and health. Too much of anything can lead to stress and anxiety.
- **Disconnect to Reconnect:** Occasionally disconnect from the digital world and the incessant noise. Spend time in nature or indulge in activities that help you reconnect with your inner self.

## Your Inner Peace, Your Power

Remember, inner peace is not a destination but a journey. It's about finding calm in the chaos, not avoiding the chaos. It is a soft yet powerful force, an inner compass guiding you towards decisions and actions aligned with your true self.

Cultivating inner peace is empowering. It enhances your ability to handle stress, boosts emotional resilience, and promotes mental well-being. It serves as the foundation for your confidence, positivity, and motivation. Embrace it, nurture it, and let it guide you on your journey toward igniting the spark within.

# CHAPTER 91: OVERCOMING PERFECTIONISM

Perfectionism, like fire, can be a beneficial servant but a destructive master. We often confuse it with the pursuit of excellence, seeing it as a noble quality that drives us to improve, innovate, and achieve. And yes, it does have a role to play in pushing us to strive for our best, but when it spirals out of control, it can become debilitating, leading to anxiety, depression, and even paralyzing inaction. This chapter of our journey together aims to help you recognize and overcome perfectionism, to swap it for a healthier approach toward goals and personal growth.

Let's start by understanding what perfectionism is. Simply put, it's a personality trait characterized by a person's striving for flawlessness and setting high-performance standards (sometimes unachievably so), often accompanied by overly critical self-evaluations and concerns or anxieties regarding others' evaluations. When we tether our self-worth to achieving perfection, we set ourselves up for consistent disappointment and distress, as the reality is that perfection is an illusion.

It's essential to differentiate between striving for excellence and being a perfectionist. The former is about setting high but achievable standards and accepting that making mistakes is a part of the learning process. The latter sets excessively high and often unrealistic goals, viewing any misstep as a catastrophic failure.

So, how can we combat perfectionism? Here are some strategies:

## 1. Develop Self-Compassion:

One of the key remedies to perfectionism is to develop self-compassion. It involves being gentle to ourselves when we encounter setbacks or make mistakes instead of mercilessly judging and criticizing ourselves for every error. Treat yourself as you would treat a friend in a similar situation.

## 2. Practice Mindfulness:

Mindfulness encourages the individual to live in the present moment and accept it without judgment. It allows you to observe your perfectionist thoughts and label them as what they are – just thoughts, not facts.

## 3. Set Realistic Goals:

It's important to aim high, but make sure your goals are realistic and achievable. Remember, perfection is not a prerequisite for success. Set goals based on your abilities and circumstances, not on a standard of perfection.

## 4. Cultivate a Growth Mindset:

With a growth mindset, you believe that abilities can be developed through dedication and hard work. This view creates a love for learning and resilience, transforming mistakes and failures into opportunities for growth.

## 5. Seek Professional Help:

If perfectionism starts to interfere with your daily life or mental health, it's crucial to seek help from a mental health professional. Cognitive Behavioral Therapy (CBT), for example, has been proven to be effective in addressing perfectionism.

**Exercise: Combating Perfectionist Tendencies**

*Exercise: Reflect on areas in your life where you might be holding onto perfectionist tendencies. Write them down and also list potential outcomes if you continue down this path. Then, using the strategies listed above, write down an action plan on how you can begin to combat these perfectionist tendencies.*

Remember, the goal is not to eliminate the drive to improve and succeed. It's about developing a healthier relationship with yourself, learning to handle failures gracefully, and understanding that your worth is not solely tied to your accomplishments. Overcoming perfectionism involves a shift from a self-defeating mindset to one of self-compassion, realistic expectations, and embracing the perfectly imperfect nature of being human.

# CHAPTER 92: REDEFINING SUCCESS FOR YOURSELF

Welcome to Chapter 92. You've made a remarkable journey so far, transforming yourself and your understanding of various facets of confidence, positivity, and motivation. This chapter, "Redefining Success for Yourself," is about dismantling societal norms of success and building a personal definition that reflects your values, dreams, and aspirations.

Success, as a concept, has been conditioned into our minds by society, media, family, and peers. It often appears as a penthouse suite, an expensive car, a high-paying job, or any other symbol of material wealth. While there's nothing inherently wrong with these things, when we allow these stereotypes to define our success, we risk ignoring our unique path and intrinsic values. We're here today to challenge this perception and help you build a personal definition of success, one that's tailor-made for your life.

## 1. Reflect on Your Values

Begin by asking yourself, "What are the values that guide me?" These could range from freedom, creativity, compassion, resilience, and family to any number of things. By understanding your core values, you'll gain clarity on what truly matters to you, which is the first step in redefining your success.

## 2. Define Your Own Success

Once you're clear on your values, it's time to define what success looks like for you. It could be the ability to spend quality time with loved ones, create art, make a positive difference in others' lives, achieve peace of mind, or any goal that aligns with your values. This is YOUR success, so ensure it's something that resonates deeply with who you are.

### 3. Set Personal Goals

Align your goals with your definition of success. They should be specific, measurable, attainable, relevant, and time-bound (SMART). Ensure these goals contribute to your overall life vision. It could be as simple as reading a book each month or as ambitious as starting your own business.

### 4. Celebrate Small Wins

Once you start achieving your goals, don't forget to celebrate, no matter how small the accomplishment may seem. Each step forward is a testament to your commitment and resilience. It helps build momentum and fuels motivation.

### 5. Regular Check-Ins

Finally, regularly revisit and revise your definition of success. Life changes, and so do you. It's important to check if your goals and definitions still resonate with you or if they need adjusting. Keep in mind that there's no fixed endpoint to success; it's an ongoing journey.

As you redefine success for yourself, you'll find a sense of fulfillment and contentment that far surpasses any external validation. Remember, you are the author of your life story, and you have the power to define how success looks in your narrative. Redefining success isn't about lowering standards; it's about raising the bar to match your highest self. It's about igniting your confidence, positivity, and motivation to chase what truly sparks joy in your life. So go forth, embrace this process, and build a life that radiates with your unique version of success.

# CHAPTER 93: HONORING YOUR PERSONAL RHYTHMS

Life moves at a frenetic pace. In the constant swirl of activities, deadlines, and commitments, it's easy to lose sight of our own natural rhythms. This chapter will guide you toward recognizing, accepting, and honoring your personal rhythms, enabling you to live a life that feels more balanced, harmonious, and true to who you really are.

## Understanding Your Personal Rhythms

Your personal rhythms are your natural patterns of energy and rest, creativity and reflection, activity and relaxation. They're unique to you – determined by your physiology, psychology, and lifestyle. Some people are morning people, feeling most alert and productive in the early hours of the day. Others are night owls, hitting their stride when the sun goes down. Some people need quiet solitude to recharge, while others draw energy from being around others.

Honoring these rhythms isn't about being selfish or inflexible. It's about understanding yourself and working with your natural tendencies rather than against them. In doing so, you'll reduce stress, increase productivity, improve your well-being, and ultimately, be more capable of giving your best to the world.

## Recognizing Your Rhythms

Take a moment to consider your own rhythms. When do you feel most energized and focused during the day? When do you find yourself needing rest or downtime? What types of activities energize you, and which ones deplete your energy?

You might find it helpful to keep a journal for a week or so, noting your energy levels, mood, and productivity at different times of the day and in different situations. Look for patterns and insights that might help you better understand your personal rhythms.

## Respecting Your Rhythms

Once you've identified your rhythms, the next step is to respect them. This doesn't mean that you can always do exactly what you want when you want – that's not the reality of life. But it does mean making conscious choices where possible that align with your natural rhythms.

If you're a morning person, can you rearrange your schedule to tackle the most challenging tasks first thing in the day? If you know you need quiet time to recharge, can you carve out pockets of solitude in your week? These shifts might seem small, but over time, they can have a big impact on your well-being.

## Nurturing Your Rhythms

Finally, honoring your personal rhythms means nurturing them. This might involve developing routines that align with your rhythms, like a morning routine that helps you start your day off right or an evening routine that helps you unwind and prepare for a good night's sleep.

It might also involve standing up for your needs when they're at odds with societal or social expectations. If you're an introvert in an extroverted world, it might mean learning to say no to some social engagements in favor of quiet time at home.

Nurturing your rhythms isn't always easy, but it's an essential part of self-care. By honoring your personal rhythms, you're acknowledging and affirming your unique needs and strengths.

You're paving the way for a life that is not just successful but also fulfilling, balanced, and joyful.

To honor your personal rhythms is to honor yourself. It's an act of self-respect, self-awareness, and self-love. And it's one of the most powerful ways you can ignite your confidence, positivity, and motivation.

## Exercise: In tune – your perfect day

*Reflect on your personal rhythms and write down your observations. Notice any changes or adjustments you could make to better honor your rhythms.*

*Plan out a 'perfect day' based on your rhythms. How would it look? How would it feel? What could you do to make this more of a reality in your everyday life?*

Remember, this is your life. Don't just dance to the beat of your own drum – honor it, nurture it, and let it lead you to a life that truly resonates with who you are.

# CHAPTER 94:
# BUILDING A POSITIVE
# LIVING SPACE

Welcome to Chapter 94 of "Spark: Ignite Your Confidence, Positivity, and Motivation." In this chapter, we will delve into the importance of building a positive living space and how it can significantly influence your confidence, positivity, and motivation. Your physical environment can be a mirror reflecting your internal state. By consciously shaping your surroundings, you can construct a place that nurtures positivity, boosts motivation, and bolsters confidence.

### The Impact of Your Living Space

Our surroundings silently communicate with us, impacting our mood, focus, creativity, and mental health. Research has demonstrated that cluttered, disorganized spaces can often lead to strong emotions of stress and anxiety, while clean, orderly spaces can promote calm and peace. In essence, the state of your physical space plays a crucial role in your psychological well-being.

### Steps to Create a Positive Living Space

Let's consider some practical ways to transform your living space into a positive and supportive environment.

**1. Decluttering:** Start by decluttering your space. This act is not just about tidiness; it's a symbolic gesture of letting go of the old to make room for the new. As you sort through physical items, you may also be processing mental clutter. The act of purging what's unnecessary can feel liberating and bring clarity to your mind.

**2. Personalization**: Next, personalize your space with objects that resonate with you and reflect your aspirations. This could be inspirational quotes, family photographs, art pieces, or souvenirs from your travels. Surrounding yourself with items that make you happy and remind you of your journey can motivate you to keep moving forward.

**3. Lighting and Colors**: Pay attention to the lighting and colors in your space. Natural light is a mood booster, so try to maximize it. When it comes to colors, choose those that evoke the emotions you wish to feel. For example, blues and greens are often associated with tranquility, while yellows and oranges can stimulate energy and creativity.

**4. Comfort and Functionality**: Make sure your space is comfortable and functional. Furniture should support the activities you frequently engage in, whether that's working, exercising, cooking, or relaxing. Comfort and convenience encourage positive habits and productivity.

**5. Incorporating Nature:** Incorporating elements of nature into your living space can have profound effects on your mental health. This could be as simple as adding a few houseplants or using natural materials and textures in your decor. The sight and smell of nature can be soothing and help reduce stress.

**6. Creating Sacred Spaces:** Finally, consider creating a "sacred" space—a dedicated area for relaxation, meditation, or any activity that brings you peace and joy. This could be a cozy reading nook, a corner filled with your favorite art supplies, or a simple meditation space with candles and cushions.

## Exercise: Reflect and Act

*Reflect on the current state of your living space. Does it support positivity and motivation? Does it reflect who you are and what you aspire to be? If not, identify one change you can make today to start transforming your living space. Remember, every small action counts.*

Creating a positive living space is a continual process of refining and aligning your surroundings to your evolving self. As you progress on your journey of confidence, positivity, and motivation, let your space evolve with you. After all, your environment is not just where you live—it's a significant part of how you live.

Next, in Chapter 95, we will explore the concept of cultivating courage in the face of fear, a critical aspect of igniting your personal 'Spark.'

# CHAPTER 95: CULTIVATING COURAGE IN THE FACE OF FEAR

"Courage is not the absence of fear, but the triumph over it." – Nelson Mandela.

Welcome to Chapter 95 of your journey. By now, you've gained an understanding of various aspects of self-belief, motivation, and positivity, and you've been introduced to a plethora of techniques to apply these concepts to your life. Today, we explore the idea of courage, specifically, how you can cultivate it in the face of fear.

Fear is a natural and universal human emotion. It's a survival mechanism that has served us since the dawn of humanity. However, in our modern world, fear often presents itself not as a response to physical danger but rather as a reaction to uncertainty, change, or perceived threats to our self-image or sense of belonging.

To harness the power of fear and transform it into courage, we must first acknowledge and understand our fears. What are you afraid of? Rejection, failure, the unknown, judgment from others? These fears are common, but remember, they're subjective and often based on our own perceptions and past experiences.

Understanding your fears allows you to challenge them. Are they truly indicative of something dangerous or damaging? Or are they distorted reflections of your self-doubt and insecurities? When you challenge your fears, you weaken their grip on you, which opens up space for courage to grow.

This courage isn't about being fearless; it's about taking action despite feeling fear. It's about making a decision that your growth, dreams, and values are more important than the discomfort of stepping into the unknown.

To cultivate courage, we need to exercise it, much like a muscle. Start small. Take steps outside of your comfort zone. Speak up in a meeting. Try a new hobby. Each act of courage, however small, strengthens your "courage muscle."

Keep in mind that each step you take is not a guarantee against failure or negative outcomes. It's not about succeeding every time; it's about cultivating resilience, learning from our experiences, and not allowing fear to dictate our actions.

A simple, practical exercise you can use to face fear and cultivate courage is the "FEAR Challenge." This is a four-step process:

**Face it:** Identify a fear that is holding you back.

**Explore it:** Investigate why this fear exists. Is it based on past experiences?

**Act despite it**: Plan a small, manageable step that moves you towards facing this fear.

**Reflect on it:** After taking this step, reflect on the experience. Was it as scary as you expected? What did you learn?

By using the FEAR Challenge regularly, you'll find your capacity for courage growing. You'll be more prepared to face bigger challenges, more resilient in the face of setbacks, and more confident in your ability to navigate through life's uncertainties. In the face of fear, courage is a choice. It's a commitment to live in alignment with your values, to embrace the unknown, and to move forward despite the challenges you may encounter. When you cultivate courage, you are taking a decisive step to ignite your confidence, positivity, and motivation.

So, fear not the journey ahead, for it is in the moments when we are most challenged that our courage shines brightest, sparking our true potential.

Take courage, dear reader. Your spark is waiting to be kindled.

# CHAPTER 96: LEARNING FROM MISTAKES

There is a famous saying by Albert Einstein, "Anyone who has never made a mistake has never tried anything new." In this chapter, we delve into the essential aspect of personal growth - learning from mistakes.

Throughout life, you will undoubtedly make mistakes, some small and forgettable, others so monumental they may alter the course of your life. Rather than seeing these moments as defeats or regrets, I invite you to see them as stepping stones towards your growth, a wellspring of lessons to be learned.

### The Power of Mistakes

Every mistake, when viewed from a positive perspective, offers a valuable learning experience. The key to gaining from these experiences is to adopt a growth mindset, as we explored in Chapter 4, recognizing that failure is an inherent part of the process toward success and growth.

Each mistake you make is a chance to refine your approach to learn more about yourself, your abilities, and how you respond to challenges. Rather than being something to fear or avoid, mistakes should be embraced as part of the journey toward reaching your goals.

### Turning Mistakes into Opportunities

How can we transform a negative event into a positive learning experience? It begins with a willingness to engage in honest self-reflection. When a mistake occurs, take time to analyze what went wrong. Was it due to a lack of preparation, a misunderstanding, or perhaps an emotional response?

Use these questions not to wallow in self-pity or self-criticism but to understand the factors that led to the mistake. This analysis will offer you insights on what to improve and how to avoid similar mistakes in the future.

### Forgiving Yourself and Moving Forward

Perhaps one of the most challenging aspects of dealing with mistakes is the process of self-forgiveness. It's easy to get caught up in cycles of self-blame and regret. However, remember that everyone, no matter how successful, makes mistakes. It is a part of being human.

Allow yourself to experience the emotions that come with mistakes – disappointment, frustration, or sadness. But do not let these feelings hold you captive. Practice self-compassion, reminding yourself that every mistake is a stepping stone towards growth.

### Lessons Are Everywhere

The beauty of learning from mistakes is that it applies to all areas of your life – personal, professional, social, or spiritual. Each context provides unique lessons that can inform your actions in the future.

To practice this, you can start a 'learning journal,' where you jot down a brief description of each significant mistake, the circumstances surrounding it, and, most importantly, what you learned from it. Review this journal periodically to remind yourself of these lessons and monitor your progress.

To help you integrate this chapter's insights into your life, I invite you to engage in the following exercise:

## Exercise: Active Learning

*Identify a mistake you made in the recent past. It can be big or small, as long as it had an impact on you. Write down what happened, why it happened, and how you felt. Reflect on what you learned from this experience and how you can use learned knowledge moving forward.*

Remember, in the journey of sparking your confidence, positivity, and motivation, every mistake is not a setback but a setup for a comeback. Keep learning, keep growing, and never lose your spark.

# CHAPTER 97: RESPECTING AND LOVING YOURSELF

As we near the conclusion of our journey, we must return to the heart of our pursuit of confidence, positivity, and motivation: the self. In this chapter, we will delve into the significance of self-respect and self-love, integral aspects of your journey that underpin all other elements of personal growth.

Self-respect and self-love are deeply intertwined. They reflect the fundamental recognition of your intrinsic worth and the deliberate care and compassion you extend toward yourself. It's about understanding your value, treating yourself kindly, and creating space for growth and acceptance.

## A. Understanding Self-Respect

The foundation of self-respect lies in the belief of your inherent worth. This is not based on your accomplishments, social status, or approval from others but on the simple fact that you are human, deserving of dignity and respect. Self-respect involves setting personal boundaries, advocating for your needs, and allowing yourself to let go of unhealthy relationships and environments.

### Exercise: Establish your boundaries
*Reflect on situations where you felt your boundaries were violated. What could you have done differently? Write down three personal boundaries you want to establish moving forward.*

## B. The Importance of Self-Love

Self-love, on the other hand, is the act of treating yourself with kindness and understanding. It's about nurturing your needs, showing compassion during your failures, and celebrating your victories. This does not mean being narcissistic or self-absorbed. It means acknowledging your worthiness of care and affection just as much as anyone else.

### Exercise: 10-minute joy
*Spend 10 minutes each day doing something that brings you joy. This simple act of self-care is a tangible expression of self-love.*

## C. The Interplay Between Self-Respect and Self-Love

Self-respect and self-love reinforce each other in a positive loop. As you practice self-respect by honoring your boundaries and values, you enhance your self-love by affirming your worth. Conversely, as you cultivate self-love through acts of self-care and positive self-talk, you bolster your self-respect by treating yourself as someone of value.

### Exercise: Self-love/Self-respect Affirmations
*Write down five affirmations that resonate with your journey of self-respect and self-love. Repeat these affirmations to yourself each morning and evening.*

## D. Cultivating Self-Respect and Self-Love

Developing self-respect and self-love is not an overnight process. It takes practice and patience. It might involve confronting past hurts, unlearning negative self-beliefs, and breaking away from societal expectations. Remember, the objective is not to attain some imagined state of perfection. It's about progressively realizing your worth and treating yourself accordingly.

### Exercise: Self-love/Self-respect Journal
*Dedicate a journal to your self-respect and self-love journey.*

*Document your experiences, feelings, triumphs, and struggles. Review this journal regularly to track your growth and remind yourself of your resilience.*

As you learn to respect and love yourself, you'll find that the world around you starts to reflect this new reality. You'll attract healthier relationships, make choices aligned with your well-being, and navigate life's challenges with greater resilience and optimism. Remember, the love and respect you have for yourself set the bar for all the relationships in your life. Ignite the spark within, and let it shine brightly, demonstrating to the world how you ought to be treated.

# CHAPTER 98: CONNECTING WITH NATURE FOR MENTAL HEALTH

The natural world around us is a reservoir of wisdom and tranquility. In the bustle of our fast-paced modern lives, we often forget our intrinsic connection to the environment that sustains us. This chapter aims to enlighten you on the power of reestablishing this connection and using it to enhance your mental health.

There's a term that you might not have heard of: 'ecotherapy.' It's the practice of spending time in nature to boost growth and healing, especially mental health. Time and again, studies have proven the therapeutic effects of nature on our mental well-being.

Remember how you felt the last time you took a walk in the woods or sat by a babbling brook? There's a chance you felt more peaceful and maybe a bit happier. This isn't a coincidence. Nature soothes us. The sound of rustling leaves, the chirping of birds, the fragrance of fresh earth after a rainfall - all of these elements engage our senses in the most gentle way, calming our mind and easing stress.

Now, let's delve into the practical ways of how you can integrate nature into your daily life for a healthier mind:

**Regular Walks** in Nature: Walking is an excellent exercise for both your body and mind. When you do it in nature, it becomes even more therapeutic. Try to take regular walks in a park or a forest or along the beach. Let your senses absorb the tranquility around you. Observe the shapes of leaves, listen to the birds, feel the texture of the tree bark, and smell the fresh air. Allow your mind to detach from its usual whirl of thoughts and become immersed in the sensory experience of nature.

**Gardening:** If you have access to a garden, use it to your advantage. Gardening is an excellent way to connect with the earth. It's a soothing, meditative practice that can also provide you with a sense of achievement as you watch your plants grow.

**Outdoor Meditation:** The practice of meditation is immensely beneficial for mental health. Doing it outdoors, in a serene natural setting, can amplify these benefits. The sounds of nature can act as a perfect backdrop for your meditation practice.

**Bring Nature Indoors:** If you reside in an urban setting with limited access to green spaces, bring nature to you. Indoor plants, nature sounds, and images of nature all can create a calming ambiance.

**Nature's Rhythms:** Try aligning your daily rhythm with that of nature. Rise with the sun, and dim the lights as sunset approaches. You'll find yourself more attuned to your natural circadian rhythm, which can promote better sleep and overall health.

**Mindful Eating:** Eating is another everyday process through which you can connect with nature. Pay attention to the food you eat. Where does it come from? How does it grow? This practice promotes gratitude towards nature and the nourishment it provides.

Remember, the idea is not to think of nature as a destination but as an integral part of your existence. It's about cultivating an ongoing relationship with the natural world. This practice can help you gain perspective, reducing stress, and enhancing your ability to stay present. So, whether you're taking a walk in the park, planting seeds, or simply enjoying a sunset, take the time to connect with nature and boost your mental well-being. The peace you seek may just be a leaf, a stone, or a cloud away.

# CHAPTER 99: PRACTICING KINDNESS TOWARDS YOURSELF AND OTHERS

After countless chapters, lessons, and reflections, we now arrive at one of the most significant points of personal growth and positivity: kindness. And when we say kindness, we're not just referring to the outward acts that we extend to others. The practice of kindness also involves being kind to ourselves. Just as we discussed the importance of self-love, self-care, and self-compassion in the previous chapters, kindness plays a significant role in these areas, creating a powerful foundation for our confidence and positivity.

## The Power of Kindness

Kindness is more than a mere virtue. It's a transformative power that can affect you and the people around you in profound ways. And what makes kindness truly powerful is its simplicity. A simple act of kindness can light up someone's day, make you feel good, and create ripples of positivity. But why is kindness so potent?

Research has shown that being kind to others has the effect of triggering a release of the hormone oxytocin, also known as the "love hormone." This not only boosts our mood but also induces feelings of warmth, euphoria, and connection with others. It's as if nature designed us to be kind.

But being kind isn't always easy. We live in a fast-paced, high-stress world where kindness is often overlooked, forgotten, or even perceived as weakness. The truth, however, couldn't be more different. Kindness is a strength, and practicing it consistently requires courage, patience, and understanding.

### Practicing Kindness to Yourself

Just like how the flight attendants instruct us to put on our oxygen mask first before helping others, practicing kindness should begin with ourselves. It's about showing empathy to our shortcomings, forgiving our mistakes, and celebrating our victories, no matter how small.

How do we start? Here are a few steps:

- Forgive yourself: Understand that everyone makes mistakes. The most important part is learning from them and moving forward.
- Practice self-care: This involves taking care of your physical, emotional, and mental well-being.
- Speak kindly to yourself: The way we talk to ourselves matters. Practice using kind, encouraging words when you're speaking to yourself.
- Celebrate your accomplishments: Acknowledge and celebrate your victories, no matter how small they may seem.

### Spreading Kindness to Others

Kindness begets kindness. By being kind to others, we cultivate a cycle of positivity that can affect the people around us, encouraging them to do the same. Here's how you can spread kindness:

Offer help: If you spot someone struggling, offer your assistance. It may be as straightforward as helping someone carry their groceries or as significant as supporting a friend going through a difficult time.

Show appreciation: Saying thank you or expressing appreciation can mean a lot to the recipient.

Be empathetic: Try to understand people's feelings and see things from their perspective.

Small acts of kindness: Simple acts like holding the door open for someone, sharing a smile, or thoughtfully giving up your seat on a crowded bus can make a big difference.

## Exercises: Practicing Kindness

*To make the act of kindness a daily habit, let's start with some exercises:*

*Kindness journal: Keep a record of all the acts of kindness you perform or witness every day.*

*Kindness challenge: Set a goal to perform at least one random act of kindness each day.*

*Meditation on kindness: Practice mindfulness and loving-kindness meditation. Visualize sending love and kindness to yourself, your loved ones, and even strangers.*

Let kindness be your guiding light, illuminating your path toward confidence, positivity, and motivation. And always remember, in a world where you can be anything, be kind.

# CHAPTER 100: EMBRACING THE JOURNEY, NOT JUST THE DESTINATION

Every step, every stumble, every success, and every setback – they're all part of your unique journey. Life is not just about reaching your destination but also about embracing and learning from the path that leads you there.

Often, we're so fixated on the end goal that we overlook the beauty and lessons of the journey. Life is in constant flux, and each moment holds a treasure trove of experiences. Embrace the uncertainty, the unknown, and the excitement that the journey brings.

This is not to discount the importance of goals. On the contrary, having a destination gives our lives direction. It provides a sense of purpose and drives us forward. Yet, the process of striving for these goals, the steps we take, and the transformations we undergo – these are equally, if not more, significant. It's in the journey where growth happens, where wisdom is gained, and where character is forged.

As you continue your path of self-discovery and personal growth, remember to find joy in the journey. Allow yourself to be present in each moment, savoring the sweetness of victories and learning from the sting of defeats. It's about not just surviving, but thriving through the ups and downs, making the most out of each experience.

You might not always have control over the outcome, but you do have control over how you react to it. Adaptability is key. It's about having the resilience to adjust your sails when the winds of life change direction. By embracing the fluidity of life, you are developing the ability 'to dance in the rain' rather than passively waiting for the storm to pass.

Each chapter of this book has been a step in your journey. From understanding the power of self-belief to practicing kindness towards yourself and others – you have covered a vast landscape of self-discovery.

Remember, progress is not linear. There will be days where you'll take two steps forward and one step back. Don't let this discourage you. Each step back is an opportunity to reassess, to learn, and to leap forward with newfound insight.

And so, as we conclude, remember: your journey is uniquely your own. No one else can walk it for you, nor should they. Cherish your individual path with its twists and turns, highs and lows. Embrace the journey with an open heart and an open mind, always recognizing the value of the process, not just the outcome.

Keep feeding the spark we have kindled together in this book. Continue igniting your confidence, positivity, and motivation. For the journey never truly ends, and the beauty lies in becoming, in evolving, in growing.

The destination may give you direction, but the journey... the journey gives you life. Embrace it, love it, and most importantly, live it. For in the journey, you'll find yourself. In the journey, you'll create yourself. Embrace the journey, not just the destination. This is where your real story lies.

So, here's to your journey - may it be beautiful, may it be enlightening, and above all, may it be truly yours. And as you navigate through it, remember that no matter the detours, no matter the obstacles, you have the power to keep the spark alive, to keep moving forward, and to keep growing, one step at a time.

# CONCLUSION: MAINTAINING YOUR SPARK – A LIFETIME JOURNEY

We've now reached the end of this illuminating journey, an exploration filled with growth, enlightenment, and learning. However, this endpoint is not truly the end. Instead, it is another beginning, another launch pad for you to take flight.

In the past 100 chapters, we've delved into the complexities and nuances of confidence, positivity, and motivation. We've dissected them, studied them, and learned ways to cultivate them. You have been presented with an assortment of tools, techniques, and insights designed to stoke the spark within you and keep it burning brightly. This Spark represents your potential, your dreams, and your power. It symbolizes the courage to venture beyond your comfort zone, the willingness to embrace challenges, and the ability to rise above adversity.

But remember, the journey of self-discovery and personal growth is never linear. It's a path filled with twists and turns, mountains and valleys, sunshine and rain. There will be times when your Spark may flicker or wane. Do not lose heart during these moments. Instead, lean into the wisdom and knowledge you've gained from this book. Reach into your toolkit and stoke your Spark until it burns bright again. Remember, maintaining your Spark is a lifelong journey, and the beauty of this journey lies in its continuity and evolution.

You have learned the power of self-belief, the significance of positivity, and the importance of motivation. You have been reminded of the importance of authenticity, resilience, humility, empathy, and gratitude. You've gained insights into the power of language, the role of body language, and the importance of embracing change and uncertainty. The value of lifelong learning and personal growth is now clear, and you know the importance of nurturing mental health, setting personal boundaries, and fostering positive relationships.

With all this knowledge and these tools at your disposal, remember to always practice kindness – towards others, but most importantly, towards yourself. Self-compassion, as we've learned, is the fuel that will keep your Spark alive and glowing.

Remember that this book is not something to be read once and then placed on a shelf. It's a reference, a guide, a friend that you can revisit anytime you need. Whenever you feel lost or unsure, come back to these pages. Revisit a chapter that resonates with you, reread a passage that brings comfort, practice an exercise that helped you before.

Each day is an opportunity for you to shine brighter, to share your warmth and light with the world. You have the tools and the knowledge; the rest is up to you. Believe in yourself, stay positive, remain motivated, and above all, keep your Spark alive. As we wrap up this journey, remember one thing: you are not defined by your destination but by the journey you undertake, the growth you experience, and the person you become. This is just the beginning. Continue to learn, to grow, and to Sparkle. As you move forward, carry this final thought with you: Embrace the journey, not just the destination, and maintain your Spark – it's a lifetime journey.

With that, dear reader, here is wishing you a journey filled with light, growth, and an eternal Spark. Ignite your confidence, positivity, and motivation, and become the best version of yourself. You have it within you. Now let the world see it.

# THE END

Printed in Great Britain
by Amazon

37274802R00159